A Network Defender's Guide to Threat Detection

Using Zeek, Elasticsearch, Logstash, Kibana, Tor, and more...

First Edition

Richard Medlin

A Network Defender's Guide to Threat Detection
Using Zeek, Elasticsearch, Logstash, Kibana, Tor, and more...
First Edition

First Edition First Published: June 1, 2020

Editors: Jeremy Martin
              Daniel Traci

The information in this book is distributed on an "As IS" basis, without warranty. The author and publisher have taken great care in preparation of this book but assumes no responsibility for errors or omissions. No liability is assumed for incidental or consequential damages in connection with or arising out of the use of the information or programs contained herein.

Rather than use a trademark symbol with every occurrence of a trademarked name, this book uses the names only in an editorial fashion and to the benefit of the trademark owner, with no intention of infringement of the trademark.

Due to the use of quotation marks to identify specific text to be used as search queries and data entry, the author has chosen to display the British rule of punctuation outside the quotes. This ensures that the quoted context is accurate for replication. To maintain consistency, this format is continued throughout the entire publication.

The writer and publisher of this article do not condone the misuse of Tor for illegal activity.

This is purely instructional for the purposes of anonymous surfing on the internet for legal usage and for testing Tor traffic monitoring in a subsequent article.

Amazon Cataloging-in-Publication Data:

ISBN-13: 979-8649104074

Contents

About the Author

Richard K. Medlin

Richard Medlin is a renowned information security author — encompassing 20 years of information security experience. His writing includes influential walk-throughs and articles in the Cyber Intelligence Report and other publications. He is a risk management expert and has been providing training and oversight — to a department of over 500 employees — for information systems for over a decade. His experience and expertise are sought out from people all over the world, and his articles focus on teaching industry experts how to investigate and minimize risks using the Risk Management Framework.

As a cyber security research and development engineer, I am currently writing about bug hunting, vulnerability research, exploitation, and digital forensic investigation. I am an author and an original developer on the first all-inclusive digital forensic investigations operating system, CSI-Linux. Collectively, I have 20 years of information security expertise and primarily focus on red and blue team operations, and digital forensics

Introduction

Have you ever found yourself questioning whether your network is in good hands? Did you do everything you could to defend against exploits on your network? Is your employer safe because you have one of the best Security Information Event Management (SIEM) setups you can use monitoring the network for you? Or, maybe you are new to Information Security and you want to learn how to employ a robust Intrusion Detection System (IDS) but you do not know where to start. If you have ever asked yourself any of these questions, or you just want to learn about ELK Stack and Zeek (Bro), you have come to the right place. A quick Google search will show you there isn't a lot of information for configuring Zeek (Bro), ElasticSearch, Logstash, Filebeat, and Kibana— it is rather complicated because the websites will describe how to install, but they don't really lead you to specifics on what else you need to do, or they are really outdated. That is where you must piece together the information yourself, and really research — lucky for you, I did the leg work for you and decided to write this book.

Whether you have been in the Information Security industry for many years or you're just getting started this book has something for you. In my time studying over the years I've always found that a lot of books are interesting reads, but they add a lot of fluff. That was not my goal with this book; I wanted to provide you with a straight forward book without the fluff, that will show you exactly what you need — I cover the basics, and then explain the intricacies involved with configuring a SIEM that is reliable. I also provide a step-by-step process, while including any pertinent notes that you need to pay attention to, and lastly providing a breakdown of what is occurring at that time. Having background to each section and knowing what is happening is extremely important to learning and understanding what is happening on your network. Likewise, this book covers a brief overview of different programming languages, and their configuration nuances when applied to Zeek (Bro) and Elk Stack. I tried my best to approach this as if you did not know anything, so that anyone can read this and understand what is happening throughout the installation and configuration process. Let us get to the basics of what will be covered in this book so that you have a good idea of what you will learn.

The first section of this book covers the Zeek(Bro) IDS installation and configuration. Furthermore, you will learn about the origin of Zeek (Bro), and the many features that Zeek (Bro) has to offer. This section will walk you through the entire installation process, while providing explanations for the configuration changes that we make on the system. There are a lot of dependencies needed to install Zeek (bro), and I will walk you through that entire process. We will also go over installing PF_ring — a tool for increased capture speeds and network capture optimization. The tool is very useful when capturing data on large networks, and from multiple nodes.

In the next section we will go over installing Tor, and Privoxy for network anonymity. You are probably asking yourself why you would want to do that when setting up a SIEM or IDS. The simple answer is that in order to know what's traversing the network, you need to understand what it is doing and how to use it yourself. Sometimes the best defense comes from knowing what the offense is using. Once we install Tor, you can generate some Tor traffic on your network, and watch as one of the custom Zeek (Bro) signatures — I will teach you about in this book — detects this traffic so you can see what it looks like once a notice is generated. It is also good to know how to remain anonymous on the network if you're ever doing any type of forensic investigations too, so learning this is always a plus.

The next section of this book will cover how to install the ELK Stack — this is the point that most walk-throughs stop, because there is a lot of custom programing and configuration involved after the initial installation process. This whole process will usually take several people, but what you learn in this book will teach you how to do the whole process from start to finish on your own. I break down the JSON and YAML files used to configure your custom ELK Stack structure, allowing the programs to interconnect and quick sort your data in an easy to view method. I explain each step of the way and try to simplify what I learned after countless hours of research. You will learn how to setup up geo location for network traffic, and how to quickly sort through thousands of logs quickly. During the last part of this section we cover some common troubleshooting issues that can arise.

Once you have everything installed and configured, we take a deep dive into actually making the IDS and SIEM useful. What good is an IDS that cannot detect anything? Custom Signatures are what Zeek (Bro) uses to provide Notices and Alerts. I will go over how to program many of the Custom Signatures that I found useful, and a description of what they do. I placed all of the signatures on GitHub for ease of install so that you can get them with a simple command. One of the most notable signatures is for detecting Tor traffic on the network. That is not always easy to do, but if you know what you're looking for — which I will show you — it's actually really simple. This can come in handy for catching malicious actors on the network. There is a total of 48 signatures that you will learn to employ, from tracking credit card information being sent clear text over the network to http attacks.

The last section of this book covers how to configure your Kibana Dashboard. The dashboard is what you use to quickly see a snapshot of what is happening on your network. Being able to quickly drill down on network connectivity issues, connections, and protocols on the network is important, and Kibana provides countless ways to view your data. The dashboard is what ties your SIEM together without having to dig through thousands of logs. Quickly identifying trends allows you to focus on the things that matter.

Once you are done reading this book, I am confident that you will be able to install, configure, and deploy an IDS and SIEM combination that will serve your needs. You will learn everything you need to know to operate Zeek (Bro) IDS, and ELK Stack to keep your network, and company's data safe. Attacks will happen, and sometimes employees will unknowingly do something on the network that could cause a liability issue but having the right tools in place will help mitigate these risks.

Zeek (Bro) IDS Installation and Configuration

Zeek (Bro) is open-source software used for network analysis. Zeek (Bro) was originally called Bro when it was introduced back in 1994 by Vern Paxon. The name came from a reference to George Orwell's Older Brother from the novel Nineteen Eighty-Four. Zeek (Bro) is a Network Intrusion Detection System (NIDS) but also provides live analysis of network events. Zeek (Bro) uses pcap to capture IP packets and transfers them to an event engine that will accept or reject them, and then it forwards the packets to a policy script interpreter.

Some useful features of Zeek (Bro) is the ability to analyze network traffic, files, or recorded network traffic — PCAP files — and it can use tracefiles to generate a neutral event; these events occur when anything on the network happens. Zeek (Bro) uses a best-guess interpretation of network events based on signatures and behavioral analysis. To install Zeek (Bro), we need to have a set of dependencies place. Zeek (Bro) also has analyzers embedded in the event engine, and the accompanying policy scripts. Furthermore, these policy scripts can be configured and edited by the user.

Zeek (Bro) has analyzers that can distinguish between HTTP, FTP, SMTP, and DNS traffic. Other analyzers can be added to detect host, port scans, and syn-floods. Zeek (Bro) software can integrate with other programs such as Snort and Elastic Search.

This section of the walkthrough will focus on installing PF_RING and Zeek (Bro).

Requirements for Zeek (Bro) Installation

Necessary libraries:

- Libcap
- OpenSSL libraries
- BIND8 library
- Libz
- Bash (for Zeek Control)
- Python 2.6 or greater (for Zeek Control)

You will need root or sudo privileges to install and set up a lot of the items in this book.

Required dependencies:

- Make
- CMake 2.8.12 or greater
- C/C++ Compiler with C++11 support
- GCC 4.8+ or Clang 3.3+
- SWIG
- Bison 2.5
- Flex
- Libcap headers
- OpenSSL headers
- zlib headers
- Python

We will cover how to install these dependencies later in the walkthrough.

Overview of this Section

- Configure Ubuntu to Effectively Capture Packets
  - Disable Network Manager
  - Disable NIC Offloading Functions
  - Enable DNS "Network" Service
  - Set the Sniffing Interface to Promiscuous Mode
- Install the Required Dependencies
- Installing Optional Dependencies
  - GeoIP Support with LibmaxMindDB and GeoLite2
  - Installing GeoLite2
  - Install PF_RING
    - Install PF_RING Kernel Modules
- Install Zeek (Bro)
  - Configuring Zeek (Bro)
  - Run Zeek (Bro)

This installation was performed on a MacBook Pro running macOS Mojave version 10.14.6 (18G95), with in Parallels Desktop 15 VM running Ubuntu Server 19.

Configure Ubuntu to effectively capture packets

Disable NetworkManager

Network Manager is a service provided by Ubuntu that manages network connections and attempts to keep the network connectivity active when it's available. It effectively manages WiFi, Ethernet, Mobile Broadband (WWAN), and PPPoE devices; Network Manager also provides VPN integration. The "NetworkManager" works well for most instances, but when we are trying to capture network data, we want the system to do this passively, so we need to turn this off. To check for the previous installation of NetworkManager on your machine perform the following steps:

1. **Run** the following commands to stop the Network Manager:

    sudo systemctl stop NetworkManager.service

    sudo systemctl disable NetworkManager.service

To restart NetworkManager change stop to start and disable to enable.

```
iwcdev@iwcdev:~$ sudo systemctl stop NetworkManager.service
[sudo] password for iwcdev:
Failed to stop NetworkManager.service: Unit NetworkManager.:
iwcdev@iwcdev:~$ sudo systemctl disable NetworkManager.serv:
Failed to disable unit: Unit file NetworkManager.service doe
iwcdev@iwcdev:~$
```

2. **Run** the following command to verify the NetworkManager has been disabled:

    sudo systemctl list-unit-files | grep NetworkManager

```
iwcdev@iwcdev:~$ sudo systemctl list-unit-files | grep NetworkManager
iwcdev@iwcdev:~$ sudo systemctl list-unit-files | grep apparmor
apparmor.service                        enabled
iwcdev@iwcdev:~$
```

I did not have the NetworkManager installed, so it returned nothing, but I changed the service to apparmor on the second line to show what it would look like if you did have NetworkManager.

Disable NIC Offloading Functions

Network Interface Card (NIC) offloading can create problems when sniffing network traffic because it can lump TCP packets together, and this will show packet sizes with an MTU larger than 1500. Some modern TCP/IP stacks lump packets to improve performance on GBPS links, but we do not want this to happen when we are analyzing network traffic. Network offloading is used by the OS and CPU to offload the work involved with transmitting packets, and sometimes it causes problems, but not always. In this case we want it turned off.

1. **Run** the following command to see what network interface you are using:

   Ifconfig

   ```
   iwcdev@iwcdev:~$ ifconfig
   enp0s5: flags=4163<UP,BROADCAST,RUNNING,MULTICAST>  mtu 1500
           inet 10.211.55.9  netmask 255.255.255.0  broadcast 10.211.55.255
           inet6 fdb2:2c26:f4e4:0:21c:42ff:fea1:9988  prefixlen 64  scopeid 0x0<global>
           inet6 fe80::21c:42ff:fea1:9988  prefixlen 64  scopeid 0x20<link>
           ether 00:1c:42:a1:99:88  txqueuelen 1000  (Ethernet)
           RX packets 9419  bytes 7542881 (7.5 MB)
           RX errors 0  dropped 0  overruns 0  frame 0
           TX packets 7016  bytes 708007 (708.0 KB)
           TX errors 0  dropped 0 overruns 0  carrier 0  collisions 0

   lo: flags=73<UP,LOOPBACK,RUNNING>  mtu 65536
           inet 127.0.0.1  netmask 255.0.0.0
           inet6 ::1  prefixlen 128  scopeid 0x10<host>
           loop  txqueuelen 1000  (Local Loopback)
           RX packets 1409  bytes 145230 (145.2 KB)
           RX errors 0  dropped 0  overruns 0  frame 0
           TX packets 1409  bytes 145230 (145.2 KB)
           TX errors 0  dropped 0 overruns 0  carrier 0  collisions 0
   ```

In this example, I am using the interface: enp0s5. Make note of your interface for use later.

2. Make sure you have ethtool installed by **running** the following commands:
   sudo apt-get update
   sudo apt-get install ethtool

Ethtool is a utility used to display and modifying parameters of the network interface controllers (NICs) and their device drivers.

```
iwcdev@iwcdev:~$ sudo apt-get update
[sudo] password for iwcdev:
Hit:1 http://es.archive.ubuntu.com/ubuntu disco InRelease
Get:2 http://es.archive.ubuntu.com/ubuntu disco-updates InRelease [97.5 kB]
Get:3 http://es.archive.ubuntu.com/ubuntu disco-backports Ir
Get:4 http://es.archive.ubuntu.com/ubuntu disco-security InF
Fetched 284 kB in 1s (393 kB/s)
Reading package lists... Done
iwcdev@iwcdev:~$ sudo apt-get install ethtool
Reading package lists... Done
Building dependency tree
Reading state information... Done
ethtool is already the newest version (1:4.19-1).
ethtool set to manually installed.
0 upgraded, 0 newly installed, 0 to remove and 0 not upgraded
iwcdev@iwcdev:~$
```

In this example I already had ethtool installed.

3. **Run** the following command to disable offloading, and **enter** your **sudo passwd**:

sudo ethtool -K enp0s5 rx off tx off tso off ufo off gso off gro off lro off

You do not want to permanently disable this on a production machine, but you can for a dedicated machine.

Make sure you replace enp0s5 with your interface

You will need to run this command every time you load Zeek (Bro) to ensure that offloading is turn off.

Set all the parameters that were changed back to on, to revert this change if needed.

Listed below are the commands you can enable or disable:

- rx - receive (RX) checksumming
- tx - transmit (TX) checksumming
- tso - TCP segmentation offload
- ufo - UDP segmentation offload
- sg - scatter gather
- gso - generic segmentation offload
- gro - generic receive offload
- rxvlan - receive (RX) VLAN acceleration
- txvlan - transmit (TX) VLAN acceleration
- lro - large receive offload
- ntuple - receive (RX) ntuple filters and actions
- rxhash - receive hashing offload

```
iwcdev@iwcdev:~$ sudo ethtool -K enp0s5 rx off tx off tso off ufo off gso off gro off lro off
[sudo] password for iwcdev:
Cannot change rx-checksumming
Cannot change udp-fragmentation-offload
Cannot change large-receive-offload
```

I received the following result stating "cannot change rx-checksumming, udp-fragmentation-offload, and large-receive-offload message."

Use the next step to make sure that these items were turned off. As you can see from my example, they were still set off.

4. **Run** the following command and use your interface to ensure everything was set off:

sudo ethtool -k enp0s5

```
iwcdev@iwcdev:~$ sudo ethtool -k enp0s5
Features for enp0s5:
rx-checksumming: off [fixed]
tx-checksumming: off
        tx-checksum-ipv4: off [fixed]
        tx-checksum-ip-generic: off
        tx-checksum-ipv6: off [fixed]
        tx-checksum-fcoe-crc: off [fixed]
        tx-checksum-sctp: off [fixed]
scatter-gather: on
        tx-scatter-gather: on
        tx-scatter-gather-fraglist: off [fixed]
tcp-segmentation-offload: off
        tx-tcp-segmentation: off
        tx-tcp-ecn-segmentation: off [fixed]
        tx-tcp-mangleid-segmentation: off
        tx-tcp6-segmentation: off
udp-fragmentation-offload: off
generic-segmentation-offload: off
generic-receive-offload: off
large-receive-offload: off [fixed]
rx-vlan-offload: off [fixed]
tx-vlan-offload: off [fixed]
ntuple-filters: off [fixed]
receive-hashing: off [fixed]
highdma: on [fixed]
rx-vlan-filter: off [fixed]
vlan-challenged: off [fixed]
tx-lockless: off [fixed]
```

Enable DNS "Network" Service

If you need to configure your own DNS, you can perform the following commands:

1. **Run** the following command:

sudo nano /etc/resolv.conf

```
# This file is managed by man:systemd-resolved(8). Do not edit.
#
# This is a dynamic resolv.conf file for connecting local clients to the
# internal DNS stub resolver of systemd-resolved. This file lists all
# configured search domains.
#
# Run "resolvectl status" to see details about the uplink DNS servers
# currently in use.
#
# Third party programs must not access this file directly, but only through the
# symlink at /etc/resolv.conf. To manage man:resolv.conf(5) in a different way,
# replace this symlink by a static file or a different symlink.
#
# See man:systemd-resolved.service(8) for details about the supported modes of
# operation for /etc/resolv.conf.

nameserver 127.0.0.53
options edns0
search localdomain
```

2. For this walkthrough, I'm not altering this file, but if your environment has a DNS server you need to add the following to the configuration file. Replace the IP with your nameserver IP:

nameserver aaa.bbb.ccc.ddd

nameserver eee.fff.ggg.hhh

```
# This file is managed by man:systemd-resolved(8). Do not edit.
#
# This is a dynamic resolv.conf file for connecting local clients to the
# internal DNS stub resolver of systemd-resolved. This file lists all
# configured search domains.
#
# Run "systemd-resolve --status" to see details about the uplink DNS servers
# currently in use.
#
# Third party programs must not access this file directly, but only through the
# symlink at /etc/resolv.conf. To manage man:resolv.conf(5) in a different way,
# replace this symlink by a static file or a different symlink.
#
# See man:systemd-resolved.service(8) for details about the supported modes of
# operation for /etc/resolv.conf.

#nameserver 127.0.0.53
nameserver 192.168.10.15
nameserver 192.168.10.20
options edns0
```

3. **Save** the file by hitting **Ctrl-x**, and then hit **y** and enter.

4. **Run** the following command to enable the network:

sudo systemctl enable network

5. **Run** the following command to restart the service:

sudo systemctl restart network

After you enable the network, you need to restart it, so the settings take effect.

Set the Sniffing Interface to Promiscuous Mode

In order for the CPU to receive all of the frames that are traveling across the network we need to configure the NIC to use promiscuous mode. Promiscuous mode allows the controller to pass all traffic it receives instead of just traffic it's programmed to receive. Essentially, this makes the NIC act as a bridge and allows all information through while only "listening" rather than making decisions.

1. **Run** the following command using your NIC, and **enter your password** when requested:

   sudo ifconfig enp0s5 promisc

2. To check that your NIC is now in promiscuous mode **run** the following command and use your NIC:

   sudo ip a show enp0s5 | grep -i promisc

```
iwcdev@iwcdev:~$ sudo ifconfig enp0s5 promisc
[sudo] password for iwcdev:
Sorry, try again.
[sudo] password for iwcdev:
iwcdev@iwcdev:~$ sudo ip a show enp0s5 | grep -i promisc
2: enp0s5: <BROADCAST,MULTICAST,PROMISC,UP,LOWER_UP> mtu 1500 qdisc fq_codel state UP
group default qlen 1000
iwcdev@iwcdev:~$
```

The first part of this command is going to show us the same information as ifconfig, but we add the " | " — called a pipe — to send that information to the grep command and grep the lines that have promisc contained. The grep command takes out the extra data we do not care about seeing right now and shows us what we specify.

Install the require Dependencies

1. To **install** the Dependencies required for Zeek (Bro), **run** the following command in the Terminal:

   sudo apt-get install cmake make gcc g++ flex bison libpcap-dev libssl-dev python-dev swig zlib1g-dev

2. **Enter** password.
3. **Press Y** to continue.

```
Do you want to continue? [Y/n] y
Get:1 http://es.archive.ubuntu.com/ubuntu disco/main amd64 m4 amd64 1.4.18-2 [199 kB]
Get:2 http://es.archive.ubuntu.com/ubuntu disco/main amd64 flex amd64 2.6.4-6.2 [317 kB]
Get:3 http://es.archive.ubuntu.com/ubuntu disco/main amd64 libpython2.7-minimal amd64 2.7.16-2 [335 kB]
Get:4 http://es.archive.ubuntu.com/ubuntu disco/main amd64 python2.7-minimal amd64 2.7.16-2 [1,310 kB]
Get:5 http://es.archive.ubuntu.com/ubuntu disco/main amd64 python2-minimal amd64 2.7.16-1 [27.8 kB]
Get:6 http://es.archive.ubuntu.com/ubuntu disco/main amd64 python-minimal amd64 2.7.16-1 [5,996 B]
Get:7 http://es.archive.ubuntu.com/ubuntu disco/main amd64 libpython2.7-stdlib amd64 2.7.16-2 [1,909 kB]
Get:8 http://es.archive.ubuntu.com/ubuntu disco/main amd64 python2.7 amd64 2.7.16-2 [244 kB]
Get:9 http://es.archive.ubuntu.com/ubuntu disco/main amd64 libpython2-stdlib amd64 2.7.16-1 [7,432 B]
Get:10 http://es.archive.ubuntu.com/ubuntu disco/main amd64 libpython-stdlib amd64 2.7.16-1 [5,828 B]
Get:11 http://es.archive.ubuntu.com/ubuntu disco/main amd64 python2 amd64 2.7.16-1 [26.5 kB]
Get:12 http://es.archive.ubuntu.com/ubuntu disco/main amd64 python amd64 2.7.16-1 [7,836 B]
Get:13 http://es.archive.ubuntu.com/ubuntu disco/main amd64 binutils-common amd64 2.32-7ubuntu4 [200 kB]
Get:14 http://es.archive.ubuntu.com/ubuntu disco/main amd64 libbinutils amd64 2.32-7ubuntu4 [468 kB]
9% [14 libbinutils 3,365 B/468 kB 1%]                              312 kB/s 4min 1s
```

You can see the list of dependencies come up, to check if the following Optional Dependencies were previously installed. If they are not, then follow the next steps.

```
The following NEW packages will be installed:
  binutils binutils-common binutils-x86-64-linux-gnu bison cmake cmake-data flex g++ g++-8 gcc gcc-8 libasan5
  libatomic1 libbinutils libbison-dev libc-dev-bin libc6-dev libcc1-0 libexpat1-dev libfl-dev libgcc-8-dev
  libitm1 libjsoncpp1 liblsan0 libmpx2 libpcap-dev libpcap0.8-dev libpython-dev libpython-stdlib libpython2-dev
  libpython2-stdlib libpython2.7 libpython2.7-dev libpython2.7-minimal libpython2.7-stdlib libquadmath0 librhash0
  libssl-dev libstdc++-8-dev libtsan0 libubsan1 libuv1 linux-libc-dev m4 make manpages-dev python python-dev
  python-minimal python2 python2-dev python2-minimal python2.7 python2.7-dev python2.7-minimal swig swig3.0
  zlib1g-dev
0 upgraded, 58 newly installed, 0 to remove and 0 not upgraded.
Need to get 79.9 MB of archives.
```

You should see the terminal prompt come back up once everything is installed.

```
Setting up zlib1g-dev:amd64 (1:1.2.11.dfsg-1ubuntu2) ...
Setting up g++-8 (8.3.0-6ubuntu1) ...
Setting up libpython2.7-dev:amd64 (2.7.16-2) ...
Setting up libpcap-dev:amd64 (1.8.1-6ubuntu1) ...
Setting up g++ (4:8.3.0-1ubuntu3) ...
update-alternatives: using /usr/bin/g++ to provide /usr/bin/c++ (c++) in auto mode
Setting up libpython2-dev:amd64 (2.7.16-1) ...
Setting up python2.7-dev (2.7.16-2) ...
Setting up python2-dev (2.7.16-1) ...
Setting up libpython-dev:amd64 (2.7.16-1) ...
Setting up python-dev (2.7.16-1) ...
Processing triggers for mime-support (3.60ubuntu1) ...
Processing triggers for gnome-menus (3.32.0-1ubuntu1) ...
Processing triggers for libc-bin (2.29-0ubuntu2) ...
Processing triggers for man-db (2.8.5-2) ...
Processing triggers for install-info (6.5.0.dfsg.1-4build1) ...
Processing triggers for desktop-file-utils (0.23-4ubuntu1) ...
iwcdev@iwcdev:~$
```

4. **Run** the following command to clean up the screen:

   clear

Install Optional Dependencies

One useful feature in Ubuntu / Debian Linux is the ability to search for a program using the apt:

apt search <dependency-name>

The apt utility is a command-lin too for installing, removing, and updating packages. This tool is used to interact with the linux packaging system. If the program is available, then you can "apt-get install" the dependency you are looking for. Please note that it is always a good idea to use google to make sure the apt search result is showing you the newest version, if not you will want to download it via a different method. You will see how this works in the following steps.

GEOIP Support with LibmaxMindDB and GeoLite2

Zeek (Bro) has the ability to use LibmaxMindDB's city or coutry database. You can sign up for an account at MaxMind. A quick google search will take you to their website, I do not want to post a link in case the web page changes. Follow along below in order to install libmaxmind using the apt utility in linux.

Installing libmaxminddb

1. Search for the libmaxmind dependency:

   apt search libmaxminddb

```
iwcdev@iwcdev:~$ apt search libmaxminddb
Sorting... Done
Full Text Search... Done
libmaxmind-db-reader-perl/disco 1.000013-2 all
  Perl module to read MaxMind DB files and look up IP addresses

libmaxmind-db-reader-xs-perl/disco 1.000007-2 amd64
  fast XS implementation of the MaxMind DB reader

libmaxminddb-dev/disco 1.3.2-1 amd64
  IP geolocation database library (development headers)

libmaxminddb0/disco 1.3.2-1 amd64
  IP geolocation database library

mmdb-bin/disco 1.3.2-1 amd64
  IP geolocation lookup command-line tool
```

2. **Run** the following command:

   sudo apt-get install libmaxminddb-dev

```
iwcdev@iwcdev:/$ sudo apt-get install libmaxminddb-dev
Reading package lists... Done
Building dependency tree
Reading state information... Done
The following NEW packages will be installed:
```

3. **Enter** your sudo **password**, and ensure you **select Y** and press **enter** if prompted during the install.

```
iwcdev@iwcdev:/$ sudo apt-get install libmaxminddb-dev
Reading package lists... Done
Building dependency tree
Reading state information... Done
The following NEW packages will be installed:
  libmaxminddb-dev
0 upgraded, 1 newly installed, 0 to remove and 0 not upgraded.
Need to get 15.6 kB of archives.
After this operation, 78.8 kB of additional disk space will be used.
Get:1 http://es.archive.ubuntu.com/ubuntu disco/universe amd64 libmaxmind
amd64 1.3.2-1 [15.6 kB]
Fetched 15.6 kB in 1s (24.4 kB/s)
Selecting previously unselected package libmaxminddb-dev:amd64.
(Reading database ... 100756 files and directories currently installed.)
Preparing to unpack .../libmaxminddb-dev 1.3.2-1 amd64.deb ...
Unpacking libmaxminddb-dev:amd64 (1.3.2-1) ...
Setting up libmaxminddb-dev:amd64 (1.3.2-1) ...
Processing triggers for man-db (2.8.5-2) ...
```

4. **Run** the following command to clear the screen:

clear

Installing GeoLite2

1. We will use the Curl command as follows to **download geolite2**:

cURL is short for "Client URL" and is a tool used to transfer data to or from a server using several different protocols. Curl is driven by libcurl for all its features and is used in the command line or scripts to perform transfer of data.

curl -o geolite2.tar.gz

"https://geolite.maxmind.com/download/geoip/database/GeoLite2-City.tar.gz"

If this link changes google geolite2 and use the new link.

```
iwcdev@iwcdev:~/Downloads$ curl -o geolite2.tar.gz "https://geolite.maxmind.com/downlo
ad/geoip/database/GeoLite2-City.tar.gz"
  % Total    % Received % Xferd  Average Speed   Time    Time     Time  Current
                                 Dload  Upload   Total   Spent    Left  Speed
100 26.3M  100 26.3M    0     0  1801k      0  0:00:14  0:00:14 --:--:-- 1787k
iwcdev@iwcdev:~/Downloads$ ls
geolite2.tar.gz
```

2. **Run** the following command to extract the file:

   tar -xzvf geolite2.tar.gz

   This command unzips the tarball.

if the unzip fails, you may have mistyped the download link. Try to download it again, and make sure you have the correct link.

```
GeoLite2-City_20190903/
GeoLite2-City_20190903/LICENSE.txt
GeoLite2-City_20190903/GeoLite2-City.mmdb
GeoLite2-City_20190903/COPYRIGHT.txt
GeoLite2-City_20190903/README.txt
```

A tarball or tarfile is a group or archive of files that are compressed together using the tar command.

3. **Move** the **GeoLite2-City.mmdb** file that we just extracted into the /usr/share/GeoIP by typing the following command and ensure your file name matches the one you downloaded (IE: the date):

   sudo mv GeoLite2-City_20190820/GeoLite2-City.mmdb /usr/share/GeoIP/GeoLite2-City.mmdb

Install PF_Ring

PF_Ring is used to improve the packet capture process and increase capture speeds. It is a packet polling tool used with the NICs by using Linux NAPI. NAPI takes the packets and copies them when they enter the NIC using a circular buffer, and then it sends it to the userland application that will then read the packets from the buffer ring. PF_Ring is used to handle a lot of network data at one time and will help you optimize your network hardware to capture packets efficiently while taking some of the load off of your CPU. Let's face it, even if you're using the best processing power you can buy it's always a good idea to lower your CPU utilization. Likewise, this allows your CPU to work harder on other tasks while still ensuring the best capture rates.

For our purposes, we are placing PF_Ring into the Opt folder because that is typically where any addon package is placed. The Opt folder normally has opt/'package name' or opt/'provider'. This is similar to windows tree with C:\Windows\Program Files\"program Name", where package is the name of the program for Linux. The "provider" name is typically the LANANA (Linux Assigned Names and Numbers Authority) name that has been registered by the vendor.

Note: Each installation differs depending on the permissions you have set on your version of Linux. Sometimes you will need to use the sudo command, or just use the sudo su command to switch to super user. You should know when the command doesn't work, and then you will need to escalate your privileges.

1. **Run** the following command for dependencies:

   sudo apt-get install bison flex

```
Reading package lists... Done
Building dependency tree
Reading state information... Done
bison is already the newest version (2:3.0.4.dfsg-1build1).
flex is already the newest version (2.6.4-6).
0 upgraded, 0 newly installed, 0 to remove and 0 not upgraded.
```

2. **Change** to the /opt **directory** by using the following command:

   cd /opt

3. **Download** PF_RING by using the following command:

   git clone https://github.com/ntop/PF_RING.git

```
Cloning into 'PF_RING'...
remote: Enumerating objects: 277, done.
remote: Counting objects: 100% (277/277), done.
remote: Compressing objects: 100% (159/159), done.
remote: Total 23366 (delta 161), reused 156 (delta 90), pack-reused 23089
Receiving objects: 100% (23366/23366), 54.52 MiB | 613.00 KiB/s, done.
Resolving deltas: 100% (17035/17035), done.
```

4. **Change** to the following **directory**:

   cd PF_RING/kernel

```
iwcdev@iwcdev:/opt$ cd PF_RING/kernel
iwcdev@iwcdev:/opt/PF_RING/kernel$
```

5. **Run** the following command to install:

   make

```
iwcdev@iwcdev:/opt$ cd PF_RING/kernel
iwcdev@iwcdev:/opt/PF_RING/kernel$ make
make -C /lib/modules/5.0.0-25-generic/build SUBDIRS=/opt/PF_RING/kernel EXTRA
_CFLAGS='-I/opt/PF_RING/kernel -DGIT_REV="\"dev:1eaf126f0d45b270428c9ce8a6b98
535d01a2d55\"" -no-pie -fno-pie' modules
make[1]: Entering directory '/usr/src/linux-headers-5.0.0-25-generic'
Makefile:223: ================= WARNING =================
Makefile:224: 'SUBDIRS' will be removed after Linux 5.3
Makefile:225: Please use 'M=' or 'KBUILD_EXTMOD' instead
Makefile:226: =========================================
  CC [M]  /opt/PF_RING/kernel/pf_ring.o
  Building modules, stage 2.
  MODPOST 1 modules
  CC      /opt/PF_RING/kernel/pf_ring.mod.o
  LD [M]  /opt/PF_RING/kernel/pf_ring.ko
make[1]: Leaving directory '/usr/src/linux-headers-5.0.0-25-generic'
iwcdev@iwcdev:/opt/PF_RING/kernel$
```

The **make** utility uses a file named makefile to compile a large program that needs to be recompiled after targets are supplied. The make command compiles object files that correspond to modified source files from the installation package.

6. **Run** the following command:

   sudo make install

   ```
   iwcdev@iwcdev:/opt/PF_RING/kernel$ sudo make install
   mkdir -p /lib/modules/5.0.0-25-generic/kernel/net/pf_ring
   cp *.ko /lib/modules/5.0.0-25-generic/kernel/net/pf_ring
   mkdir -p /usr/include/linux
   cp linux/pf_ring.h /usr/include/linux
   /sbin/depmod 5.0.0-25-generic
   iwcdev@iwcdev:/opt/PF_RING/kernel$
   ```

7. **Run** the following command and enter the sudo password:

   sudo insmod ./pf_ring.ko enable_tx_capture=0 min_num_slots=32768

8. **Run** the following command:

   cd ../userland
   ls

   insmod is short for "Insert module." The Insert module is a utility that loads the specified kernel modules into the kernel.

   ```
   iwcdev@iwcdev:/opt/PF_RING/kernel$ cd ../userland
   iwcdev@iwcdev:/opt/PF_RING/userland$ ls
   c++            examples     go     libpcap-1.8.1  nbpf     tcpdump
   configure      examples_ft  lib    Makefile       nbroker  tcpdump-4.9.2
   configure.in   examples_zc  libpcap modules        snort    wireshark
   iwcdev@iwcdev:/opt/PF_RING/userland$ █
   ```

9. **Run** the following command:

   make

```
gcc  -O2  -DHAVE_PF_RING -Wall -Wno-unused-function -I../../kernel -I../lib -
I../libpcap -Ithird-party `../lib/pfring_config --include` -D HAVE_PF_RING_FT
 fttest.o ../libpcap/libpcap.a   ../lib/libpfring.a ../libpcap/libpcap.a   ..
/lib/libpfring.a `../lib/pfring_config --libs` `../libpcap/pcap-config --addi
tional-libs --static` -lpthread  -lrt -ldl -lrt -o fttest
make[1]: Leaving directory '/opt/PF_RING/userland/examples_ft'
cd wireshark/extcap; make
make[1]: Entering directory '/opt/PF_RING/userland/wireshark/extcap'
gcc  -O2  -O2 -DHAVE_PF_RING -Wall -I../../../kernel -I../../lib -I../../libp
cap -Ithird-party `../../lib/pfring_config --include` -D ENABLE_BPF -D HAVE_P
F_RING_ZC -O2  -c ntopdump.c -o ntopdump.o
gcc  -O2  -O2 -DHAVE_PF_RING -Wall -I../../../kernel -I../../lib -I../../libp
cap -Ithird-party `../../lib/pfring_config --include` -D ENABLE_BPF -D HAVE_P
F_RING_ZC -O2  ntopdump.o ../../libpcap/libpcap.a   ../../lib/libpfring.a ../
../libpcap/libpcap.a   ../../lib/libpfring.a `../../lib/pfring_config --libs`
 -lpthread  -lrt -ldl  -lrt -o ntopdump
make[1]: Leaving directory '/opt/PF_RING/userland/wireshark/extcap'
iwcdev@iwcdev:/opt/PF_RING/userland$ █
```

At this point, you will see the installation process. Now we need to install the latest version of PF_RING libraries and the kernel module:

Install PF_RING Kernel Modules

1. **Change** to the /opt/PF_RING/userland/lib **directory** by running the following:

   cd lib

   ```
   iwcdev@iwcdev:/opt/PF_RING/userland$ cd lib
   iwcdev@iwcdev:/opt/PF_RING/userland/lib$ █
   ```

2. **Run** the following command:

   ./configure --prefix=/opt/PF_RING

   ```
   iwcdev@iwcdev:/opt/PF_RING/userland/lib$ ./configure --prefix=/opt/PF_RING
   checking for gcc... gcc
   checking whether the C compiler works... yes
   checking for C compiler default output file name... a.out
   checking for suffix of executables...
   checking whether we are cross compiling... no
   checking for suffix of object files... o
   ```

3. **Run** the following command:

   make

```
iwcdev@iwcdev:/opt/PF_RING/userland/lib$ make
make -C ../nbpf
make[1]: Entering directory '/opt/PF_RING/userland/nbpf'
lex scanner.l
gcc -Wall -fPIC -O2 -I../lib -I../../kernel  -Wno-address-of-packed-member   -c
 -o lex.yy.o lex.yy.c
gcc -Wall -fPIC -O2 -I../lib -I../../kernel  -Wno-address-of-packed-member   -c
 -o grammar.tab.o grammar.tab.c
gcc -Wall -fPIC -O2 -I ../lib -I ../ /kernel  -Wno-address-of-packed-member   -c
```

4. **Run** the following command:

   make install

```
iwcdev@iwcdev:/opt/PF_RING/userland/lib$ make install
ar x ../nbpf/libnbpf.a
cp ../nbpf/nbpf.h .
ar x libs/libpfring_zc_x86_64.a
ar x libs/libpfring_ft_x86_64_dl.a
ar x libs/libpfring_nt_x86_64.a
ar x libs/libpfring_myricom_x86_64.a
ar x libs/libpfring_dag_x86_64.a
ar x libs/libpfring_fiberblaze_x86_64.a
ar x libs/libpfring_accolade_x86_64.a
ar x libs/libpfring_netcope_x86_64.a
```

5. **Performing** the following:

   cd ../libpcap

6. **Run** the following command:

   ./configure --prefix=/opt/PF_RING

```
iwcdev@iwcdev:/opt/PF_RING/userland/libpcap$ ./configure --prefix=/opt/PF_RING
checking build system type... x86_64-unknown-linux-gnu
checking host system type... x86_64-unknown-linux-gnu
checking target system type... x86_64-unknown-linux-gnu
checking for gcc... gcc
checking whether the C compiler works... yes
checking for C compiler default output file name... a.out
checking for suffix of executables...
checking whether we are cross compiling... no
checking for suffix of object files... o
```

7. **Run** the following command:

make

```
iwcdev@iwcdev:/opt/PF_RING/userland/libpcap$ make
gcc -fvisibility=hidden -fpic -I. -I ../../kernel -I ../lib  -DBUILDING_PCAP -I
HAVE_CONFIG_H  -D_U_="__attribute__((unused))" -DHAVE_PF_RING  -g -O2    -c ./
cap-linux.c
gcc -fvisibility=hidden -fpic -I. -I ../../kernel -I ../lib  -DBUILDING_PCAP -I
HAVE_CONFIG_H  -D_U_="__attribute__((unused))" -DHAVE_PF_RING  -g -O2    -c ./
cap-usb-linux.c
./pcap-usb-linux.c: In function 'usb_stats_linux':
./pcap-usb-linux.c:738:32: warning: '%s' directive output may be truncated wri
ing up to 4095 bytes into a region of size 230 [-Wformat-truncation=]
     "Can't open USB stats file %s: %s",
                                ^~

     string, strerror(errno));
     ~~~~~~
In file included from /usr/include/stdio.h:867,
                 from ./pcap/pcap.h:54,
                 from ./pcap-int.h:37
```

8. **Run** the following command:

make install

```
iwcdev@iwcdev:/opt/PF_RING/userland/libpcap$ make install
VER=`cat ./VERSION`; \
MAJOR_VER=`sed 's/\([0-9][0-9]*\)\..*/\1/' ./VERSION`; \
gcc -shared -Wl,-soname,libpcap.so.$MAJOR_VER \
    -o libpcap.so.$VER pcap-linux.o pcap-usb-linux.o pcap-netfilter-linux.o fad-getad.o pcap
.o inet.o fad-helpers.o gencode.o optimize.o nametoaddr.o etherent.o savefile.o sf-pcap.o sf
-pcap-ng.o pcap-common.o bpf_image.o bpf_dump.o  scanner.o grammar.o bpf_filter.o version.o
   ../lib/libpfring.a -lpthread -lrt   -lrt -ldl
[ -d /opt/PF_RING/lib ] || \
    (mkdir -p /opt/PF_RING/lib; chmod 755 /opt/PF_RING/lib)
```

9. **Run** the following command:

cd ../tcpdump-4.9.2

10. **Run** the following command:

./configure –prefix=/opt/PF_RING

```
iwcdev@iwcdev:/opt/PF_RING/userland/libpcap$ cd ../tcpdump-4.9.2
iwcdev@iwcdev:/opt/PF_RING/userland/tcpdump-4.9.2$ ./configure --prefix=/opt/PF_RING
checking build system type... x86_64-unknown-linux-gnu
checking host system type... x86_64-unknown-linux-gnu
checking for gcc... gcc
checking whether the C compiler works... yes
checking for C compiler default output file name... a.out
checking for suffix of executables...
checking whether we are cross compiling... no
checking for suffix of object files... o
```

11. **Run** the following command:

make

```
iwcdev@iwcdev:/opt/PF_RING/userland/tcpdump-4.9.2$ make
```

12. **Run** the following command:

make install

```
iwcdev@iwcdev:/opt/PF_RING/userland/tcpdump-4.9.2$ make install
gcc -ffloat-store -DHAVE_CONFIG_H   -D_U_="__attribute__((unused))" -DHAVE_PF_RING -I. -I../
libpcap-1.8.1  -g -O2 -c ./setsignal.c
gcc -ffloat-store -DHAVE_CONFIG_H   -D_U_="__attribute__((unused))" -DHAVE_PF_RING -I. -I../
libpcap-1.8.1  -g -O2 -c ./tcpdump.c
if grep GIT ./VERSION >/dev/null; then \
        read ver <./VERSION; \
        echo $ver | tr -d '\012'; \
        date + %Y_%m_%d; \
else \
        cat ./VERSION; \
fi | sed -e 's/ */const char version[] = "&";/' > version.c
```

13. **Run** the following command:

cd ../../kernel

14. **Run** the following command:

Make

```
iwcdev@iwcdev:/opt/PF_RING/kernel$ make
make -C /lib/modules/5.0.0-25-generic/build SUBDIRS=/opt/PF_RING/kernel EXTRA_CFLAGS='-I/opt
/PF_RING/kernel -DGIT_REV="\"dev:1eaf126f0d45b270428c9ce8a6b98535d01a2d55\"" -no-pie -fno-pi
e' modules
make[1]: Entering directory '/usr/src/linux-headers-5.0.0-25-generic'
Makefile:223: ================== WARNING ==================
Makefile:224: 'SUBDIRS' will be removed after Linux 5.3
Makefile:225: Please use 'M=' or 'KBUILD_EXTMOD' instead
Makefile:226: ============================================
  Building modules, stage 2.
  MODPOST 1 modules
make[1]: Leaving directory '/usr/src/linux-headers-5.0.0-25-generic'
iwcdev@iwcdev:/opt/PF_RING/kernel$
```

15. **Run** the following command:

sudo make install

```
iwcdev@iwcdev:/opt/PF_RING/kernel$ sudo make install
[sudo] password for iwcdev:
mkdir -p /lib/modules/5.0.0-25-generic/kernel/net/pf_ring
cp *.ko /lib/modules/5.0.0-25-generic/kernel/net/pf_ring
mkdir -p /usr/include/linux
cp linux/pf_ring.h /usr/include/linux
/sbin/depmod 5.0.0-25-generic
iwcdev@iwcdev:/opt/PF_RING/kernel$
```

16. **Run** the following command:

modprobe pf_ring enable_tx_capture=0 min_num_slots=32768

17. **Run** the following command to ensure it took:

modinfo pf_ring

```
root@iwcdev:/home/iwcdev# modprobe pf_ring enable_tx_capture=0 min_num_s
lots=32768
root@iwcdev:/home/iwcdev# modinfo pf_ring
filename:        /lib/modules/5.0.0-25-generic/kernel/net/pf_ring/pf_ring
.ko
alias:           net-pf-27
version:         7.5.0
description:     Packet capture acceleration and analysis
author:          ntop.org
license:         GPL
srcversion:      9F1D15A5A8D4F13840ACF26
depends:
retpoline:       Y
name:            pf_ring
vermagic:        5.0.0-25-generic SMP mod_unload
parm:            min_num_slots:Min number of ring slots (uint)
parm:            perfect_rules_hash_size:Perfect rules hash size (uint)
parm:            enable_tx_capture:Set to 1 to capture outgoing packets (
uint)
parm:            enable_frag_coherence:Set to 1 to handle fragments (flow
```

Configure pf_ring

1. **Run** the following commands:

   mkdir /etc/pf_ring/

   sudo touch /etc/pf_ring/pf_ring.conf

2. **Run** the following command:

   echo "min_num_slots=32768" > /etc/pf_ring/pf_ring.conf

You might need to add file permission to the pf_ring.conf file located in the /etc/pf_ring/ directory: (ex: chmod 666 or 777)

Install Zeek (Bro)

1. **Change** to the /tmp **directory** by running the following command:

   cd /tmp

2. **Run** the following command to **switch** to **super user do**, and **enter passwd**:

   sudo su

3. **Run** the following command to download Zeek (Bro):

   git clone --recursive **https://github.com/zeek/zeek**

   ```
   root@iwcdev:/tmp# git clone --recursive https://github.com/zeek/zeek
   Cloning into 'zeek'...
   remote: Enumerating objects: 79, done.
   remote: Counting objects: 100% (79/79), done.
   remote: Compressing objects: 100% (49/49), done.
   Receiving objects:   7% (8093/115607), 1.63 MiB | 651.00 KiB/s
   ```

4. **Change directory** to the Zeek (Bro) folder:

   cd zeek

   you can run the ./configure --help command to view all the options you can assign to cater this build to what you want it to do.

5. **Run** the following command:

   ./configure --with-pcap=/opt/PF_RING
   --with-geoip=/usr/share/GeoIP --prefix=/opt/zeek/

```
root@iwcdev:/tmp/zeek# ./configure --with-pcap=/opt/RF_RING --with-geoip=/usr/sh
are/GeoIP --prefix=/opt/zeek/

====================| Zeek Build Summary |====================

Build type:          RelWithDebInfo
Build dir:           /tmp/zeek/build
Install prefix:      /opt/zeek
Zeek Script Path:    /opt/zeek/share/zeek
Debug mode:          false

CC:                  /usr/bin/cc
CFLAGS:               -Wall -Wno-unused -O2 -g -DNDEBUG
CXX:                 /usr/bin/c++
CXXFLAGS:             -Wall -Wno-unused -std=c++11 -O2 -g -DNDEBUG
CPP:                 /usr/bin/c++

ZeekControl:         true
Aux. Tools:          true

libmaxminddb:        true
Kerberos:            false
gperftools found:    false
         tcmalloc:   false
         debugging:  false
jemalloc:            false

=====================================================================

-- Configuring done
-- Generating done
-- Build files have been written to: /tmp/zeek/build
```

6. **Run** the following command:

make

You do not have to use the Libmaxminddb by enabling GeoIP, this is just what I chose to use for this build.

```
root@iwcdev:/tmp/zeek# make
make -C build all
make[1]: Entering directory '/tmp/zeek/build'
make[2]: Entering directory '/tmp/zeek/build'
make[3]: Entering directory '/tmp/zeek/build'
Scanning dependencies of target binpac_lib
make[3]: Leaving directory '/tmp/zeek/build'
make[3]: Entering directory '/tmp/zeek/build'
[  0%] Building CXX object aux/binpac/lib/CMakeFiles/binpac_lib.dir/binpac_buffer.cc.o
[  1%] Building CXX object aux/binpac/lib/CMakeFiles/binpac_lib.dir/binpac_bytestring.cc.o
[  1%] Building CXX object aux/binpac/lib/CMakeFiles/binpac_lib.dir/binpac_regex.cc.o
[  1%] Linking CXX shared library libbinpac.so
make[3]: Leaving directory '/tmp/zeek/build'
[  1%] Built target binpac_lib
make[3]: Entering directory '/tmp/zeek/build'
[  1%] [FLEX][PACScanner] Building scanner with flex 2.6.4
[  1%] [BISON][PACParser] Building parser with bison 3.3.2
Scanning dependencies of target binpac
make[3]: Leaving directory '/tmp/zeek/build'
make[3]: Entering directory '/tmp/zeek/build'
```

7. **Run** the following command:

This takes a while to compile.

   make install

8. **Run** the following 2 commands:

   echo "$PATH:/opt/zeek/bin" > /etc/environment

   export PATH=/opt/zeek/bin:$PATH

```
root@iwcdev:/opt/zeek/bin# echo "$PATH:/opt/zeek/bin" > /etc/environment
root@iwcdev:/opt/zeek/bin# export PATH=/opt/zeek/bin:$PATH
root@iwcdev:/opt/zeek/bin#
```

9. **Run** the following command at the terminal:

   reboot

1. **Change** to the opt/zeek/etc **directory** and

   cd /opt/zeek/etc

2. run the following command:

   sudo nano node.cfg

3. **Edit** the **node config file** to your configuration. I changed the following for this
   setup:

```
[manager]
type=manager
host=localhost
#
[proxy-1]
type=proxy
host=localhost
#
[worker-1]
type=worker
host=localhost
interface=ens0p5
lb_method=pf_ring
lb_procs=5
```

```
#[worker-2]
#type=worker
#host=localhost
#interface=eth0

Save modified buffer?  (Answering "No" will DISCARD changes.)
Y  Yes
N  No                    ^C Cancel
```

4. **Hit ctrl-x** to exit. Type **Y** and hit **enter**.

---

*Note: You need to setup the appropriate interfaces within your node.cfg file; use the
interfaces that we found earlier using ifconfig. You may have to add lines and erase the #
out of lines. This will all be dependent on what you are doing and what your setup is like. In
order to use the lb_method, which stands for load balancing, you need to use workers. If
you run stand alone, you won't be able to set those parameters. You will see within the
config file what I mean.*

5. **Save** the file as **node.cfg** and hit enter.

6. The following command to edit the networks.cfg, ensure you are in the opt/zeek/etc directory, or whichever directory you saved Zeek (Bro) in.

sudo nano networks.cfg

```
# List of local networks in CIDR notation, optionally followed by a
# descriptive tag.
# For example, "10.0.0.0/8" or "fe80::/64" are valid prefixes.

10.0.0.0/8              Private IP space
172.16.0.0/12           Private IP space
192.168.0.0/16          Private IP space
10.211.55.0/24          Private IP space
```

.

> *Note: Enter the IP space you are working within, and use CIDR notation, and you can write optional descriptions to make it easy to remember, if you want to block out any address range, place a # to the left of the line*

If you want to edit the scripts that Zeek (Bro) uses, you can use # at the beginning of the line and turn the script on or turn off scripts by placing a # next to the line portion that has @. I left these alone during this walk through. I just want you to see that there is an option to do so.

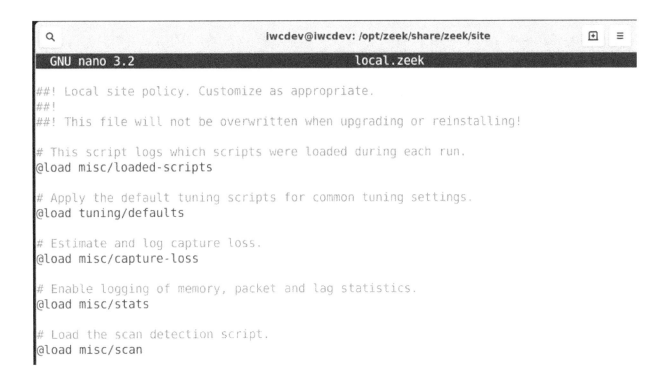

Run Zeek (Bro)

1. Run the following command to give Zeek (Bro) binaries permission to capture packets:

   sudo setcap cap_net_raw,cap_net_admin=eip /opt/zeek/bin/zeek

   sudo setcap cap_net_raw,cap_net_admin=eip /opt/zeek/bin/zeekctl

```
iwcdev@iwcdev:~$ sudo setcap cap_net_raw,cap_net_admin=eip /opt/zeek/bin/zeek
iwcdev@iwcdev:~$ sudo setcap cap_net_raw,cap_net_admin=eip /opt/zeek/bin/zeekctl
iwcdev@iwcdev:~$
```

2. To start Zeek (Bro) perform the following command:

   sudo zeekctl

   or

   sudo ./zeekctl

```
root@iwcdev:/opt/zeek/etc# zeekctl
Hint: Run the zeekctl "deploy" command to get started.

Welcome to ZeekControl 2.0.0-6

Type "help" for help.
```

You only need to run install the first time using Zeek (Bro).

3. Then **run** the following command:

   Install

```
[ZeekControl] > install
creating policy directories ...
installing site policies ...
generating cluster-layout.zeek ...
generating local-networks.zeek ...
generating zeekctl-config.zeek ...
generating zeekctl-config.sh ...
[ZeekControl] >
```

4. Then **run** the following command:

   deploy

```
[ZeekControl] > deploy
checking configurations ...
installing ...
removing old policies in /opt/zeek/spool/installed-scripts-do-not-touch/site ..
removing old policies in /opt/zeek/spool/installed-scripts-do-not-touch/auto ..
creating policy directories ...
installing site policies ...
generating cluster-layout.zeek ...
generating local-networks.zeek ...
generating zeekctl-config.zeek ...
generating zeekctl-config.sh ...
```

5. To ensure Zeek (Bro) is running perform the following command:

status

```
[ZeekControl] > status
Name        Type     Host       Status    Pid    Started
manager     manager  localhost  running   8283   27 Aug 14:06:37
proxy-1     proxy    localhost  running   8330   27 Aug 14:06:38
worker-1-1  worker   localhost  running   8422   27 Aug 14:06:40
worker-1-2  worker   localhost  running   8431   27 Aug 14:06:40
worker-1-3  worker   localhost  running   8434   27 Aug 14:06:40
worker-1-4  worker   localhost  running   8423   27 Aug 14:06:40
worker-1-5  worker   localhost  running   8436   27 Aug 14:06:40
[ZeekControl] >
```

6. **Run** the following command to permanently save the zeekctl launch command.

nano ~/.profile

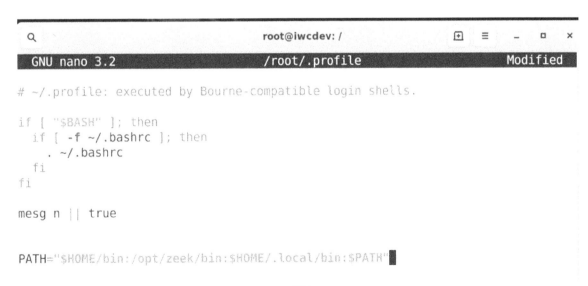

```
GNU nano 3.2                    /root/.profile                    Modified

# ~/.profile: executed by Bourne-compatible login shells.

if [ "$BASH" ]; then
  if [ -f ~/.bashrc ]; then
    . ~/.bashrc
  fi
fi

mesg n || true

PATH="$HOME/bin:/opt/zeek/bin:$HOME/.local/bin:$PATH"
```

7. Add the following line to the .profile file:

PATH="$HOME/bin:/opt/zeek/bin:$HOME/.local/bin:$PATH"

8. Run the following command to see if Zeek (Bro) is working:

tail -f /opt/zeek/logs/current/conn.log

You should see a similar output as the following picture.

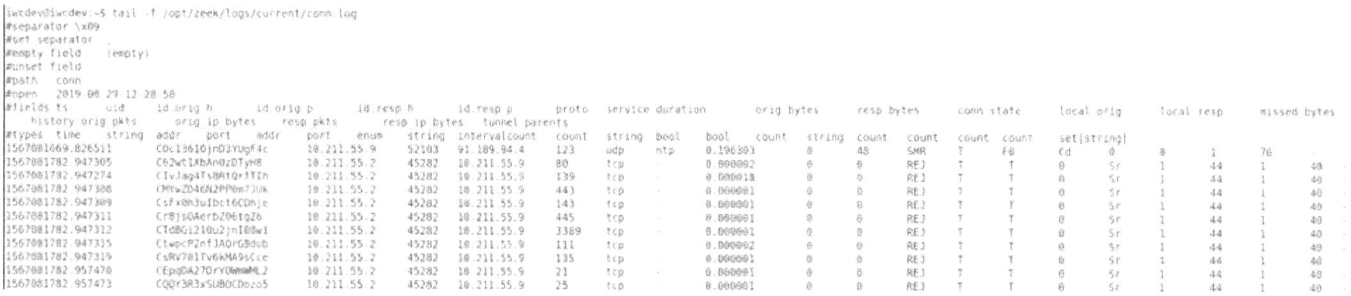

This concludes our Zeek, and PF_ring installation and usage walkthrough! For this walkthrough we covered how to configure Ubuntu for capturing packets, installed the required dependencies, and performed the successful installation of pf_ring and Zeek (Bro).

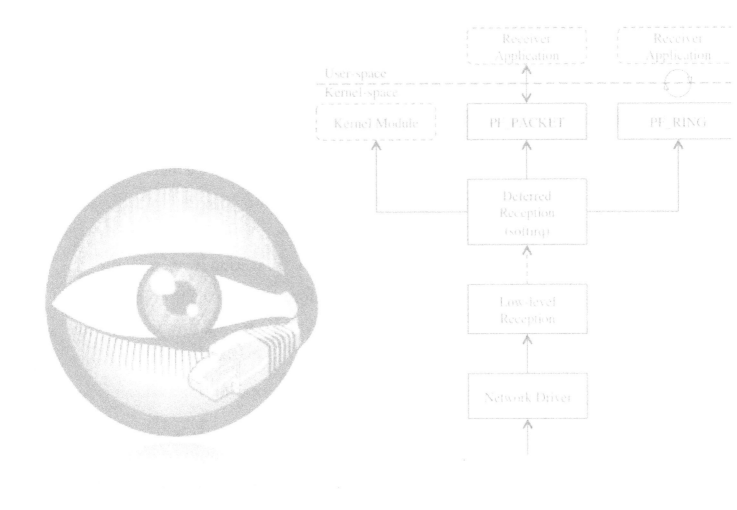

In the next section we are going to talk about Tor and install it. I know you're asking yourself, why would we install Tor when we are working with ELK stack, and Zeek. To answer your question, we are going to cover a set of signatures that you can use to start your SIEM and monitor traffic on the network. It's important to know what traffic could be potentially bad. I have included a signature that will detect tor traffic on the network. If you are seeing Tor traffic on your network, there is a very high probability that something malicious is taking place, or something that a user might not want you to see. In a business setting there usually isn't a reason you would want a user on the network tunneling their traffic through Tor. Tor can allow people to exfiltrate data or hide their identity and location while doing illegal activity.

Tor

Tor is arguably the most prominent tool for browsing the internet while providing privacy and anonymity. There are several methods for staying anonymous on the internet, and Tor's Onion routing method, is one of the most successful methods available. Onion routing is the method of ensuring the contents of data transmissions is encrypted during routing until it reaches the exit node while hiding the source of the transmission. Onion routing works by establishing a connection from point A to the destination at point B, but it takes several detours along the way using an encrypted chain of relays that is referred to as "onion routing." The network communications from point to point down the chain are encrypted, and each node is a relay, and each relay only knows which relay it received information from, and which relay it is sending to next. In theory, this method will make it harder to figure out where the transmission came from after it has passed through multiple relays. Tor communications use an encrypted private network path, called a "circuit," and creates several layers using relays. The "Onion method" proves to be an effective way of hiding the transmitting hosts identity, and the contents of the transmission. Tor used with additional proxies, and VPNs make it even harder for network communications to be deciphered.

Tor uses volunteers and sponsors to establish the relays, and new users to Tor can opt to join the Tor network as a relay. Tor's communications are considered low latency because the Tor network creates its own private network path, called a circuit, rather than stick to the shortest path method utilized by most Internet Service Providers. The last relay in the communication path in the Tor network is referred to as the "exit relay." All network connections in the Tor network are encrypted from the first relay to the exit relay.

Please be aware that if you choose to be part of the Tor network and host relays, that running an exit relay can have some legal implications. Exit relays are the last interface from the Tor network onto the internet, and any activity that is legal, or illegal is carried from the exit relay to its final destination. Tor is not always used for innocent network transmissions, so it is advised that exit relays are ran by hosting companies and not hosted personally at a household. Furthermore, you should notify your Internet Service Provider about potential issues that could come from hosting an exit relay.

Tor has several uses for criminal investigations and is commonly used by Law Enforcement (LE) agencies. Tor allows LE to surf the web without leaving any trace which is important to protect their identity from suspecting criminals. It is easy for the host of an illegal web site to check logs for IP addresses, and if multiple connections from a government IP address were detected it would tip off the suspect that there may be an ongoing investigation into their illegal activity. Likewise, Tor is also used for sting operations to keep LE anonymous when conducting web transactions. Tor can also be used by LE for "tip lines" because they allow users to remain anonymous and this fosters a trusting environment for potential informants.

Please remember, before you surf the web using Tor that you should not conduct illegal activity. If you are trying to remain anonymous do not login to your email, social media accounts, or any other identifying internet accounts. If you are simply using Tor for location obscurity, and encryption in order to be security conscious then Tor is a great tool. If you want to remain anonymous you need to remember to shy away from any actions that can be used to identify you while using Tor.

This walk through is going to cover how to Install and configure Tor, Privoxy, and Tor Browser. You will also learn how to use a script that can be made to turn on Tor, and the Tor Services, or turn it off with a simple command. The reason we are going over this is because it is important to see what Tor traffic looks like later, and we will configure a signature to detect it on your network. In order for you to see how that works, you need to have a computer that is running tor.

This install will cover the following:

- Installing Tor
- Installing Privoxy
- Installing Tor Launching Script
- Using Tor and Privoxy
- Create a Script to Toggle Tor Circuit and Services On and Off
- Give Users Permission to Start the Tor Service Without Sudo Password
- Install Tor Browser

Installing Tor

This method of installing Tor uses your general network proxy to use SOCKS proxy and is applied to the system, and not just a specific browser. SOCKS can be configured two ways. The first way to use SOCKS is within the application, and the second way is to configure a global SOCKS proxy configuration that uses an external wrapper to force the application to use socks. Setting up the proxy will be covered in the Using Tor and Privoxy section of this walk-through.

1. **Run** the following command to install **apt-transport-https** and enter your sudo password:

   sudo apt install apt-transport-https curl

   This is performed so that you can get the repository key using https repositories using the curl command.

2. **Run** the following command for root user functions:

   sudo -i

3. **Run** the following commands to **add** the **Tor Repository** to the **sources.list.d** file:

```
echo "deb deb.torproject.org/torproject.org/ $(lsb_release -cs) main" >
/etc/apt/sources.list.d/tor.list
```

4. **Run** the following command to **download** the **tor key**:

```
curl
deb.torproject.org/torproject.org/A3C4F0F979CAA22CDBA8F512EE8CBC9E88
6DDD89.asc | gpg --import
```

```
root@iwcdev:~# curl https://deb.torproject.org/torproject.org/A3C4F0F979CAA22CDBA8F512EE8CBC9E886DDD89
.asc | gpg --import
gpg: directory '/root/.gnupg' created
gpg: keybox '/root/.gnupg/pubring.kbx' created
  % Total    % Received % Xferd  Average Speed   Time    Time     Time  Current
                                 Dload  Upload   Total   Spent    Left  Speed
100 19665  100 19665    0     0  16497      0  0:00:01  0:00:01 --:--:-- 16497
gpg: key EE8CBC9E886DDD89: 36 signatures not checked due to missing keys
gpg: /root/.gnupg/trustdb.gpg: trustdb created
gpg: key EE8CBC9E886DDD89: public key "deb.torproject.org archive signing key" imported
gpg: Total number processed: 1
gpg:               imported: 1
gpg: no ultimately trusted keys found
root@iwcdev:~#
```

5. **Run** the following command to **add** the **gpg key**:

```
gpg --export A3C4F0F979CAA22CDBA8F512EE8CBC9E886DDD89 | apt-key add
-
```

6. **Run** the following command to update **Advanced Package Tool (APT)**:

```
apt update
```

```
root@iwcdev:~# apt update
Hit:1 http://es.archive.ubuntu.com/ubuntu disco InRelease
Get:2 http://es.archive.ubuntu.com/ubuntu disco-updates InRelease [97.5 kB]
Get:3 http://es.archive.ubuntu.com/ubuntu disco-backports InRelease [88.8 kB]
Get:4 http://es.archive.ubuntu.com/ubuntu disco-security InRelease [97.5 kB]
Hit:5 https://artifacts.elastic.co/packages/7.x/apt stable InRelease
```

> Note: APT is a tool used in the Terminal in Linux that allows for dpkg packaging system to manage software installations. APT is preferred of the standalone dpkg manager because it is user friendly and will install, update / upgrade, or remove packages.

7. **Run** the following command to install **Tor**, **tor-geoipdb**, **torsocks**, and the **deb.torproject.org-keyring**:

   sudo apt install tor tor-geoipdb torsocks deb.torproject.org-keyring

```
root@iwcdev:~# sudo apt install tor tor-geoipdb torsocks deb.torproject.org-keyring
Reading package lists... Done
Building dependency tree
Reading state information... Done
Suggested packages:
  mixmaster torbrowser-launcher socat tor-arm apparmor-utils obfs4proxy
The following NEW packages will be installed:
  deb.torproject.org-keyring tor tor-geoipdb torsocks
0 upgraded, 4 newly installed, 0 to remove and 4 not upgraded.
Need to get 2,437 kB of archives.
After this operation, 12.9 MB of additional disk space will be used.
Get:1 http://es.archive.ubuntu.com/ubuntu disco/universe amd64 torsocks amd64 2.3.0-1 [61.1 kB]
Get:2 https://deb.torproject.org/torproject.org disco/main amd64 deb.torproject.org-keyring all 2018
.08.06 [4,922 B]
Get:3 https://deb.torproject.org/torproject.org disco/main amd64 tor amd64 0.4.1.6-1~disco+1 [1,425
kB]
Get:4 https://deb.torproject.org/torproject.org disco/main amd64 tor-geoipdb all 0.4.1.6-1~disco+1 [
946 kB]
Fetched 2,437 kB in 13s (189 kB/s)

Selecting previously unselected package deb.torproject.org-keyring.
(Reading database ... 295285 files and directories currently installed.)
```

Installing Privoxy

Privoxy is a web proxy that filters web page data and HTTP headers to remove adds and other unwanted content.

1. **Run** the following command to install **Privoxy**:

   sudo apt install privoxy

   and

   press yes to continue

```
root@iwcdev:~# sudo apt install privoxy
Reading package lists... Done
Building dependency tree
Reading state information... Done
The following additional packages will be installed:
  doc-base libuuid-perl libyaml-tiny-perl
Suggested packages:
  rarian-compat
The following NEW packages will be installed:
  doc-base libuuid-perl libyaml-tiny-perl privoxy
0 upgraded, 4 newly installed, 0 to remove and 4 not upgraded.
Need to get 617 kB of archives.
After this operation, 2,716 kB of additional disk space will be used.
Do you want to continue? [Y/n]
```

2. **Run** the following command to **edit** the **Privoxy Config** file:

   sudo nano /etc/privoxy/config

3. **Paste** the following line at the very end of the config:

   forward-socks5 / localhost:9050 .

The period is intended after this line, so ensure you have the space and period at the end.

```
  GNU nano 3.2                            /etc/privoxy/config

#close-button-minimizes 1
#
#
#   The "hide-console" option is specific to the MS-Win console
#   version of Privoxy. If this option is used, Privoxy will
#   disconnect from and hide the command console.
#
#hide-console
#
#
forward-socks5 / localhost:9050 .
```

4. **Hash** (#) out the **logfile logfile** line in the **/etc/privoxy** config:

```
#       operating systems support log rotation out of the box, some
#       require additional software to do it. For details, please
#       refer to the documentation for your operating system.
#
logfile logfile
#
#   2.8. trustfile
#   ================
#
```

```
#        require additional software to do
#        refer to the documentation for yo
#
#logfile logfile
#
#  2.8. trustfile
#  ===============
#
#  Specifies:
```

5. **Run** the following commands to save, and exit the file:

   press "ctrl and X"
   press "Y"

   Do not change the file name.

   press "Return"

6. **Run** the following command to restart the Privoxy Service:

   sudo systemctl restart privoxy

Using Tor and Privoxy

1. **Run** the following command to ensure the Tor service is running:

   sudo systemctl start tor

2. To use **torsocks** with a specific program just use the following command:

   torsocks program_name

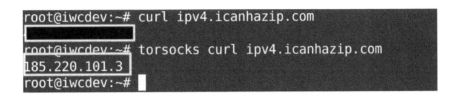

If you received an error running the torsocks command, the tor service may need to be turned on. It is worth noting that attempting to run **torsocks firefox**, or **torsocks google-chrome** will not work with the command line tool, so you will need to perform the following steps to manually enable tor socks5 proxy.

The following steps require network manager; if you do not have Network Manager installed run the following command:

apt-get install network-manager

```
root@iwcdev:~# apt-get install network-manager
Reading package lists... Done
Building dependency tree
Reading state information... Done
The following packages were automatically installed and are no longer required:
    linux-image-5.0.0-25-generic linux-modules-5.0.0-25-generic
    linux-modules-extra-5.0.0-25-generic
Use 'apt autoremove' to remove them.
The following additional packages will be installed:
    dns-root-data dnsmasq-base libbluetooth3 libmbim-glib4 libmbim-proxy libndp0
```

3. **Go to Settings** and Perform the following:

Click Network

Click the Manual Icon in the Network Proxy settings area

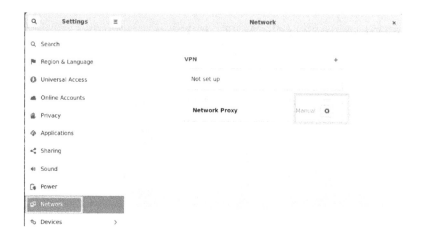

4. Under the **Network Settings** and **Network Proxy settings configure** the following:

Click Manual

Enter **Localhost** and change the port to **9050** in the Socks Host configuration box.

Leave everything else the same.

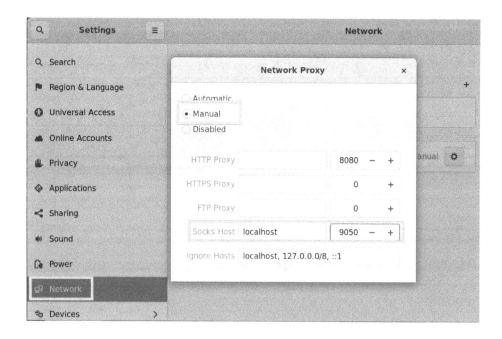

5. **Perform** the following commands to restart the **NetworkManager**, and **Tor** services:

systemctl restart NetworkManager.service

systemctl restart tor

```
root@iwcdev:~# systemctl restart NetworkManager.service
root@iwcdev:~# systemctl restart tor
root@iwcdev:~#
```

6. **Go to** the following web address to see if your tor is working correctly after setting up the manual Proxy:

check.torproject.org

Congratulations. This browser is configured to use Tor.

Your IP address appears to be: **51.75.71.123**

`

If you want to disable Tor, you can go back into the proxy settings and change it from manual to none. If you want to be able to turn off the proxy setting by performing a command at the terminal, then follow the next part of this walk through.

Create a Script to Toggle Tor Proxy and Services On and Off

> *Note: You should see an output similar to this one, but with a different IP address. This is how you will know if Tor is working correctly. Ensure the IP address showing is not your actual IP address prior to running Tor.*

1. **Run** the following command to change directory to the /bin directory:

   cd /usr/bin

   Ensure you are still the Super User before starting the following steps.

2. **Run** the following command to create **torswitch.**

   nano torswitch

3. **Paste** the following information into the file:

   #!/bin/bash

   case "$(gsettings get org.gnome.system.proxy mode)" in
   '"none"') gsettings set org.gnome.system.proxy mode '"manual"'
   echo "Tor Enabled" && sudo systemctl start tor && sudo systemctl start privoxy;;
   '"manual"') gsettings set org.gnome.system.proxy mode '"none"'
   echo "Tor Disabled" && sudo systemctl stop tor && sudo systemctl stop privoxy ;;
   esac

```
  GNU nano 3.2                       torswitch                        Modified
#!/bin/bash

case "$(gsettings get org.gnome.system.proxy mode)" in
"'none'") gsettings set org.gnome.system.proxy mode "'manual'"
echo "Tor Enabled" && sudo systemctl start tor && sudo systemctl start privoxy;;
"'manual'") gsettings set org.gnome.system.proxy mode  "'none'"
echo "Tor Disabled" && sudo systemctl stop tor && sudo systemctl stop privoxy ;;
esac
```

1. **Run** the following commands to save, and exit the file:

   press "ctrl and X"

   press "Y"

   Do not change the file name.

   press "Return"

> *Note: Regular system users that do not have permission to start services will have to use*
> *the Sudo account password when running the script to start the services. The next section*
> *in this walk-through will show you a work around to add users to the sudoer file to allow*
> *execution of services without having to enter sudo password.*

4. **Run** the following command to give the file execute privileges:

   chmod a+x /usr/bin/torswitch

5. **Run** the following command to turn the Tor Proxy, and services on and off:

   torswitch
   ```
   root@iwcdev:/usr/bin# torswitch
   Tor Disabled
   root@iwcdev:/usr/bin# torswitch
   Tor Enabled
   root@iwcdev:/usr/bin#
   ```

6. **Run** the following command to see the status of the Tor Service and ensure the script is working properly:

sudo systemctl status tor

```
root@iwcdev:/usr/bin# torswitch
Tor Disabled
root@iwcdev:/usr/bin# torswitch
Tor Enabled
root@iwcdev:/usr/bin# systemctl status tor
● tor.service - Anonymizing overlay network for TCP (multi-instance-master)
   Loaded: loaded (/lib/systemd/system/tor.service; enabled; vendor preset: enab
   Active: active (exited) since Sun 2019-11-03 20:57:12 EST; 3min 14s ago
  Process: 3699 ExecStart=/bin/true (code=exited, status=0/SUCCESS)
 Main PID: 3699 (code=exited, status=0/SUCCESS)

Nov 03 20:57:12 iwcdev systemd[1]: Starting Anonymizing overlay network for TCP
Nov 03 20:57:12 iwcdev systemd[1]: Started Anonymizing overlay network for TCP (
lines 1-8/8 (END)
```

When you start Tor with Super User, the .cache/dconf cache ownership is taken by the Super User. If you switch to a regular system user, you will see an error similar to the following picture. The Tor service will still work, but you'll see these errors. If you did not start the Torswitch program with a Root or Super User account, then you won't see this error when using Tor as a regular user, but you will need to enter the sudo password to start the service if your user doesn't have permission.

The output should show the tor services are off if the output says, "Tor Disabled." Likewise, it should say active if "Tor Enabled."

- 50 -

```
iwcdev@iwcdev:/usr/bin$ torswitch

(process:3922): dconf-CRITICAL **: 21:21:41.163: unable to create file '/home/iw
cdev/.cache/dconf/user': Permission denied.  dconf will not work properly.

(process:3922): dconf-CRITICAL **: 21:21:41.163: unable to create file '/home/iw
cdev/.cache/dconf/user': Permission denied.  dconf will not work properly.

(process:3925): dconf-CRITICAL **: 21:21:41.166: unable to create file '/home/iw
cdev/.cache/dconf/user': Permission denied.  dconf will not work properly.

(process:3925): dconf-CRITICAL **: 21:21:41.166: unable to create file '/home/iw
cdev/.cache/dconf/user': Permission denied.  dconf will not work properly.

(process:3925): dconf-CRITICAL **: 21:21:44.177: unable to create file '/home/iw
cdev/.cache/dconf/user': Permission denied.  dconf will not work properly.

(process:3925): dconf-WARNING **: 21:21:44.177: failed to commit changes to dcon
f: Could not connect: Connection refused
Tor Enabled
iwcdev@iwcdev:/usr/bin$
```

Giving Users Permission to start the Tor Service without Sudo Password

If you want to allow a user to be able to use the Tor Script without the Sudo password that normal wouldn't have permissions to run Root level commands perform the steps below. In this part of the walk-through we are going to use visudo to edit the sudoer file. The sudoer file is very sensitive to improper syntax, so you do not want to edit it on your own just in case you make a mistake. Use visudo because it will validate the syntax before saving. Failure to use proper syntax in the sudoer file can render your system useless because it can make it impossible to gain elevated privileges after you make a mistake.

1. **Run** the following command to open the temporary sudoer file using visudo:

    visudo

2. Enter the following information to allow IWC dev to start, stop, and check the status of the Tor Service, and to start the service without needing a password:

username ALL = /etc/init.d/tor

username ALL = NOPASSWD: /etc/init.d/tor

username ALL = /bin/systemctl start tor

username ALL = /bin/systemctl stop tor

username ALL = /bin/systemctl restart tor

username ALL = /bin/systemctl status tor

username ALL = NOPASSWD: /bin/systemctl start tor

username ALL = NOPASSWD: /bin/systemctl stop tor

username ALL = NOPASSWD: /bin/systemctl restart tor

username ALL = NOPASSWD: /bin/systemctl status tor

```
Q                                    root@iwcdev: /bin
GNU nano 3.2                          /etc/sudoers.tmp
iwcdev ALL = /etc/init.d/tor
iwcdev ALL = NOPASSWD: /etc/init.d/tor
iwcdev ALL = /bin/systemctl start tor
iwcdev ALL = /bin/systemctl stop tor
iwcdev ALL = /bin/systemctl restart tor
iwcdev ALL = /bin/systemctl status tor
iwcdev ALL = NOPASSWD: /bin/systemctl start tor
iwcdev ALL = NOPASSWD: /bin/systemctl stop tor
iwcdev ALL = NOPASSWD: /bin/systemctl restart tor
iwcdev ALL = NOPASSWD: /bin/systemctl status tor
```

3. Enter the following information to allow IWC dev to start, stop, and check the status of the Privoxy Service, and to start the service without needing a password:

username ALL = /etc/init.d/privoxy

username ALL = NOPASSWD: /etc/init.d/privoxy

username ALL = /bin/systemctl start privoxy

username ALL = /bin/systemctl stop privoxy

username ALL = /bin/systemctl restart privoxy

username ALL = /bin/systemctl status privoxy

username ALL = NOPASSWD: /bin/systemctl start privoxy

username ALL = NOPASSWD: /bin/systemctl stop privoxy

username ALL = NOPASSWD: /bin/systemctl restart privoxy

username ALL = NOPASSWD: /bin/systemctl status privoxy

```
iwcdev ALL = /etc/init.d/privoxy
iwcdev ALL = NOPASSWD: /etc/init.d/privoxy
iwcdev ALL = /bin/systemctl start privoxy
iwcdev ALL = /bin/systemctl stop privoxy
iwcdev ALL = /bin/systemctl restart privoxy
iwcdev ALL = /bin/systemctl status privoxy
iwcdev ALL = NOPASSWD: /bin/systemctl start privoxy
iwcdev ALL = NOPASSWD: /bin/systemctl stop privoxy
iwcdev ALL = NOPASSWD: /bin/systemctl restart privoxy
iwcdev ALL = NOPASSWD: /bin/systemctl status privoxy
```

Ensure to replace username with the actual username you are setting these permissions for.

Run the following commands to save, and exit the file:

press "ctrl and X"

press "Y"

If you need to put multiple users just keep adding the lines and replacing the username.

NOTE: DO NOT CHANGE THE FILE NAME

press "Return"

Install Tor Web Browser

The Tor Web Browser routes traffic through the Tor network and encrypts the network traffic protecting it from surveillance and analysis similar.

1. **Run** the following command to **install** the **Tor Browser**:

   sudo apt-get install torbrowser-launcher

2. **Press Y** to continue and hit return.

Note: If you did not go through the steps of installing the Tor Proxy, you need to go back to the beginning section and install the Tor Proxy.

3. **Run** the following command from the Terminal to **launch Tor**:

   torbrowser-launcher

You can't run this command as a Root user. If you are still the root user run the following command, and then go back to step 3.

4. **Run** the following command and **replace iwcdev** with your regular user account if you're currently using a root account:

su iwcdev

Repeat step 3 and then skip to step 5.

You will see a download box, then a screen should pop up saying connect to Tor up top.

```
root@iwcdev:/usr/bin# su iwcdev
iwcdev@iwcdev:/usr/bin$ torbrowser-launcher
Tor Browser Launcher
By Micah Lee, licensed under MIT
version 0.3.1
```

5. **Click Connect**.

6. **Go-to** the following URL to check and see if your browser is correctly using tor:

   check.torproject.org

Congratulations. This browser is configured to use Tor.

Your IP address appears to be: **64.71.142.240**

Please refer to the Tor website for further information about using Tor safely. You are now free to browse the Internet anonymously. For more information about this exit relay, see: Relay Search.

Donate to Support Tor

Tor Q&A Site | Volunteer | Run a Relay | Stay Anonymous

> *Note: The Tor Browser should work even if you have not run the "torswitch" script. Please note that the browser only uses Tor through the browser, so for any other communications you need to use the "torswitch" script to enable the global Tor proxy.*

This concludes our walk-through for setting up Tor. We learned how to install and configure Tor, Privoxy, and Tor Browser. Remember that using Tor is only as good at covering your tracks as you allow it to be. If you log into websites, applications, or services that you normally would use in everyday life, you can easily be identified even though your transmissions are encrypted and relayed through the Tor network.

In the next section we will go over the installation and configuration process for how to ingest the Zeek (Bro) logs into Elasticsearch using Filebeat, Logstash, and lastly, setting up Kibana to visualize the data. We will learn how to create a very powerful setup using IDS and network monitoring for use with many different types of network monitoring infrastructures. This setup will effectively function as a Security Information Event Monitoring system (SIEM).

Elastic Stack (ELK) and Zeek (Bro)

The Elastic Stack is often referred to as the ELK Stack and is a software suite made by Elastic. The ELK Stack is used to ingest data from many sources and in many different formats giving the end user a way to visualize and analyze the data instantly. Elastic products are open source and highly customizable allowing for customization in many different environments. The heart of Elastic Stack is Elasticsearch which is used to search for and analyze data using a Lucene style full-text search engine. Elasticsearch can be used on a single node or hundreds of nodes and it will still perform the same way.

Elasticsearch scales horizontally allowing for it to manage a high number of events allowing it to easily manage how the data is distributed across the cluster. Elasticsearch receives its data by ingesting it from shipping metrics within apps that they refer to as "Beats." In this installation we are going to use Filebeat to send data from Zeek to Elasticsearch via the built in Zeek Module contained within Filebeat. Alternatively, we are going to configure Filebeat to send logs to Logstash for use with a data collection pipeline that can be used to view data from several programs besides just the Zeek IDS. Elasticsearch uses a program called Kibana to visualize the data that is ingested and indexed within the Elasticsearch cluster.

Kibana provides real-time visualization of the data that Elasticsearch indexes. You can create heat maps, waffle charts, and graphs to give presentations, or simply provide a method to manage and monitor data. The great thing about Kibana is you can use it to show trends quickly and efficiently without having to dig through large amounts of logs manually.

Logstash processes data through a pipeline that is ingested from multiple sources simultaneously, and then it manipulates that data however you decide before sending it to Elasticsearch. The great part about Logstash is that you can change the way the data is parsed, and how you view it within Kibana. Logstash supports input from a wide array of sources, and can manage data from web applications, logs, metrics, AWS services and it can stream the data real time. Furthermore, Logstash can use structured and unstructured data with grok, which is a term used by Elastic that means it can parse unstructured data and translate it into structured allowing for you to be able to perform queries. Grok works well for data that is not a regular expression and you can use the dissect option for data that is reliable and repeated.

GeoIP is a feature used in Elasticsearch that uses GeoLite2 to decipher geo coordinates from IP addresses. GeoLite2 is the IP geolocation database used in both Logstash and Elasticsearch, but this method only shows a location area and does not pinpoint the IP to a specific address. IP Geolocation shows a radius based off a latitude and longitude. We will use Geoip for Logstash, and the Zeek Module to show where traffic outside the network is coming from.

Filebeat is the lightweight shipper we will use for shipping logs from Zeek (Bro) in this walkthrough. Filebeat allows you to send thousands of logs from servers, Virtual Machines, and containers allowing for centralization of the data. Filebeat uses an aggregated format that you can visualize real-time in Kibana. Furthermore, the beauty of Filebeat is the fact that it comes with several internal modules that are already preconfigured to handle logs from several popular applications that simplifies the collection and parsing of data. Filebeat also has dashboards that are preconfigured with popular examples of data analyzers that are displayed with-in Kibana dashboards. Another great feature that Filebeat offers is the ability to slow down the speed that it sends logs to Logstash or Elasticsearch; This feature is called the "backpressure-sensitive protocol" and either program will notify Filebeat to slow down sending data while it is processing, and will notify Filebeat to continue shipping information once it has caught up.

For this walkthrough we are going to go over how to install, and configure Elasticsearch, Filebeat, Kibana, and Logstash to ingest logs from Zeek (Bro) to perform analyzation and real-time monitoring. The installation process was extremely straight forward when installing these programs, and the Elastic website offers a plethora of documentation for customization and configuring.

The configuration portion of ELK is a bit more difficult because there are so many possibilities for how to ingest data, and adding in pipelines, formatting, and displaying data.

Before we start the walk through, I just want to give you a little background on how the experience went for me personally. I have never used, installed, or configured Zeek (Bro), or the ELK stack prior to this write up. I went into this scenario as a beginner, and at first the whole installation went off without a hitch. If you do a google search and look for other installation walkthroughs you will quickly notice that most stop after the installation is complete. Many of the installations will have different methods for using and configuring Filebeat and Logstash. When I started working on this project, I wanted to be able to use Zeek (Bro) and ELK together in order to have the entire functionality of GeoIP, and analyzation. It seemed like it would be pretty simple at first, and the documentation on the website goes into great detail on concepts. However, I'm not a programmer so as a newcomer it took a lot of time to research and see how these modules work together, and how the configuration works to make things happen the way I wanted. Also, I had a few hiccups with Logstash being indexed properly into Elasticsearch, which you will see in more detail in the alternate installation portion of this write-up.

My goal here is to explain some of the things I learned during this trial and error process and also show how to perform this process for any user of any skill level. The configuration files for the ELK stack are written in YAML Ain't Markup Language (YAML or YML), and JavaScript Object Notation (JSON). YML coding uses spaces for indentation, not tabs, and Elastic uses 2 spaces per indentation level on their default configuration files and Elastic recommends users to use the same format. In order to test your YML files you can run the following command to make sure you do not have any sytanx errors:

filebeat test config -c NAME_OF_FILE.yml

Use single quotation marks when using regular expressions because this will help work around YAML's string escaping issues. It is also recommended by Elastic to use single quotation marks when using paths. YAML's parser has issues identifying numeric fields that have a zero (0) for the first character, so use single quotation marks when using numbers like 07; YAML will convert this number to a float if you neglect single quotes.

The JSON filter plugin is a parsing filter built into Logstash that is used to display data from fields that are made with JSON and expands them for use as a Logstash event. If this event fails it will display _jsonparsefailure, and the data will remain untouched. The JSON files are setup similar to the YML files by using the two-space convention. The following are JSON filter plugin options:

For the add_tag option you can specify as many tags as needed, or just use one.

```
filter {
JSON {
  source => "message"
  target => "doc"
  add_field => { "foo_%{a_field}" => "Some text, from %{host}" }
   add_tag => [ "foo_%{some_other_field}" , "a second_tag_if_needed" ]
id => "XYZ"
remove_field =>  { "foo_%{a_field}" => "Some text, from %{host}" }
remove_tag => [ "foo_%{some_other_field}" , "a second_tag_if_needed" ]
```

Overview

- Preconfiguring NIC to Use Promiscuous Mode
- Installing Elasticsearch
    - Enable journalctl Logging
    - Install OpenJDK
- Install Logstash
    - Starting the Logstash Service
- Install Kibana
- Install Filebeat
- Configuring Elasticsearch and Kibana
- Post Install Configuration
    - Kibana Configuration
    - Elasticsearch Configuration
    - Filebeat Configuration
    - Zeek (Bro) Configuration
- Using the Kibana Zeek (Bro) Module to view Zeek (Bro) IDS Logs
    - Configuring the Zeek Overview Dashboard
- Alternative ELK Stack method
    - Configure Zeek (Bro) to Use JSON Output
    - Configure Logstash
    - Configure Filebeat
- Viewing Logstash GEOIP Information in Kibana
- Troubleshooting Logs in Kibana
- Conclusion

Preconfigure the NIC to use Promiscuous Mode

1. **Run** the following command:

   ethtool -K enp0s5 rx off tx off tso off ufo off gso off gro off lro off

   ```
   root@iwcdev:/# ethtool -K enp0s5 rx off tx off tso off ufo off gso off gro off l
   ro off
   Cannot change rx-checksumming
   Cannot change udp-fragmentation-offload
   Cannot change large-receive-offload
   root@iwcdev:/#
   ```

2. **Run** the following **2** commands to enable promiscuous mode and ensure you use your specific network adapter name (I used enp0s5):

   sudo ifconfig enp0s5 promisc

   sudo ip a show enp0s5 | grep -I promisc

   ```
   root@iwcdev:/# sudo ifconfig enp0s5 promisc
   root@iwcdev:/# sudo ip a show enp0s5 | grep -i promisc
   2: enp0s5: <BROADCAST,MULTICAST,PROMISC,UP,LOWER_UP> mtu 1500 qdisc fq_codel sta
   te UP group default qlen 1000
   root@iwcdev:/#
   ```

Note: The first command enables promiscuous mode for your network adapter, and the second command shows you if the network adapter is running in promiscuous mode. Likewise, if you run the second command and do not get an output then you are not in promisc mode. The "ip a" command shows an output similar to ifconfig normally, but we used the | "pipe" to send that output to the next command "grep" and used grep to show lines that contained "promisc" in order to cut out the clutter.

Installing Elasticsearch

Please take note that when you install ELK, the whole stack needs to be the same version. They have already released version 7.4. I wrote this walkthrough using 7.3.1 and 7.4 was release during editing; the installation steps are still the same.

1. **Download** and **install** the **public signing key** by using the following command:

   wget -qO - artifacts.elastic.co/GPG-KEY-elasticsearch | sudo apt-key add -

2. **Install** the **APT repository** using the following command:

   sudo apt-get install apt-transport-https

```
iwcdev@iwcdev:~$ sudo apt-get install apt-transport-https
Reading package lists... Done
Building dependency tree
Reading state information... Done
The following NEW packages will be installed:
  apt-transport-https
0 upgraded, 1 newly installed, 0 to remove and 2 not upgraded.
Need to get 1,692 B of archives.
After this operation, 155 kB of additional disk space will be used.
Get:1 http://es.archive.ubuntu.com/ubuntu disco-updates/universe amd64 apt-trans
port-https all 1.8.1 [1,692 B]
Fetched 1,692 B in 0s (7,351 B/s)
Selecting previously unselected package apt-transport-https.
(Reading database ... 100778 files and directories currently installed.)
Preparing to unpack .../apt-transport-https_1.8.1_all.deb ...
Unpacking apt-transport-https (1.8.1) ...
Setting up apt-transport-https (1.8.1) ...
```

3. **Run** the following command to add the elastic repository to your sources list:

   echo "deb artifacts.elastic.co/packages/7.x/apt stable main" | sudo tee -a /etc/apt/sources.list.d/elastic-7.x.list

```
iwcdev@iwcdev:~$ echo "deb https://artifacts.elastic.co/packages/7.x/apt stable
main" | sudo tee -a /etc/apt/sources.list.d/elastic-7.x.list
deb https://artifacts.elastic.co/packages/7.x/apt stable main
iwcdev@iwcdev:~$ 
```

4. **Run** the following command and **enter** your sudo password:

   sudo apt-get update && sudo apt-get install elasticsearch

5. **Run** the following command to configure Elasticsearch to start automatically:

   sudo /bin/systemctl daemon-reload

6. **Run** the following command to enable the elasticsearch.service:

   sudo /bin/systemctl enable elasticsearch.service

```
iwcdev@iwcdev:~$ sudo /bin/systemctl enable elasticsearch.service
Synchronizing state of elasticsearch.service with SysV service script with /lib/systemd/
systemd-sysv-install.
Executing: /lib/systemd/systemd-sysv-install enable elasticsearch
Created symlink /etc/systemd/system/multi-user.target.wants/elasticsearch.service → /lib
/systemd/system/elasticsearch.service.
```

7. **Run** the following command to start the Elasticsearch service:

   sudo systemctl start elasticsearch.service

Note: Elasticsearch does not provide feedback once the service is started. To see whether the service has successfully started you need to look at the log files in the /var/log/elasticsearch/ folder. By default, Elasticsearch doesn't log info in the system journal, so we need to enable it. Perform the following steps to enable journalctl logging:

Enable journalctl Logging

1. **Run** the following command to switch to Super User and **enter** the SU password:

   sudo su

2. **Change Directory** to the /lib/systemd/system/ folder:

   cd /lib/systemd/system/

3. **Run** the following command to edit the elasticsearch.service file:

   nano elasticsearch.service

4. **Run** the following command to change directory to /lib/system/system:

   cd /lib/systemd/system

5. **Run** the following command to edit the elasticsearch.service file:

   nano elasticsearch.service

6. **Remove** the **--quiet** option from the ExecStart setting in the elasticsearch.service file. Below I have removed it, your file should look the same.

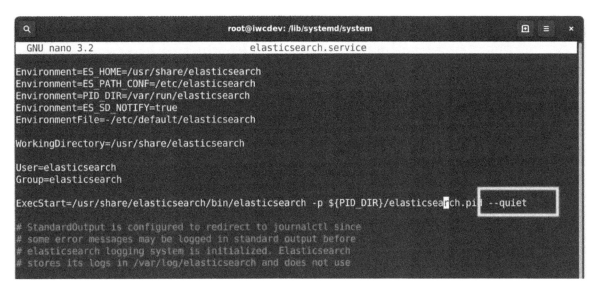

7. **Run** the following commands to save, and exit the file:

press "ctrl and X"

press "Y"

NOTE: DO NOT CHANGE THE FILE NAME.

press "Return"

8. Go back through steps 5 through 7 of the Elasticsearch install section and then **run** this command to see if the service started:

sudo journalctl --unit elasticsearch

You should see an output similar to this.

```
Aug 31 13:27:46 iwcdev systemd[1]: Started Elasticsearch.
Aug 31 13:27:46 iwcdev elasticsearch[4447]: OpenJDK 64-Bit Server VM w
Aug 31 14:11:24 iwcdev systemd[1]: Stopping Elasticsearch...
Aug 31 14:11:24 iwcdev systemd[1]: elasticsearch.service: Succeeded.
Aug 31 14:11:24 iwcdev systemd[1]: Stopped Elasticsearch.
Aug 31 14:11:24 iwcdev systemd[1]: Started Elasticsearch.
Aug 31 14:11:25 iwcdev elasticsearch[5010]: OpenJDK 64-Bit Server VM wa
Aug 31 14:11:43 iwcdev systemd[1]: elasticsearch.service: Current comma
```

If you want to see if the service has been started since a specific timeframe you can perform the following command.

sudo journalctl --unit elasticsearch --since "2019-08-31 14:19:16"

```
root@iwcdev:/lib/systemd/system# sudo journalctl --unit elasticsearch --since "
2019-10-31 20:20:20"
-- Logs begin at Sat 2019-08-24 11:52:34 EDT, end at Mon 2019-10-07 22:23:29 ED
-- No entries --
lines 1-2/2 (END)
```

There are other cli options, just use the "man journalctl" command to view them.

9. To check that the Elasticsearch program is running use the following command:

    curl -X GET 'localhost:9200/?pretty'

    or

    curl -X GET "localhost:9200/?pretty"

    or

    curl 127.0.0.1:9200

NOTE: You should get a similar output to the following. I tried multiple ways and sometimes using single quotes will work, but not dual quotes and vice versa.

```
root@iwcdev:/lib/systemd/system# curl -X GET "localhost:9200/?pretty"
{
  "name" : "iwcdev",
  "cluster_name" : "elasticsearch",
  "cluster_uuid" : "GjjvPBhWQPa4jkaEY_ENrw",
  "version" : {
    "number" : "7.3.1",
    "build_flavor" : "default",
    "build_type" : "deb",
    "build_hash" : "4749ba6",
    "build_date" : "2019-08-19T20:19:25.651794Z",
    "build_snapshot" : false,
    "lucene_version" : "8.1.0",
    "minimum_wire_compatibility_version" : "6.8.0",
    "minimum_index_compatibility_version" : "6.0.0-beta1"
  },
  "tagline" : "You Know, for Search"
}
root@iwcdev:/lib/systemd/system# █
```

You should see an output similar to the following:

You can also enter the following address in your web browser to see if Elasticsearch is running: 127.0.0.1:9200.

1. **Run** following command will also show if Elasticsearch is running:

   systemctl status elasticsearch

```
root@iwcdev:/lib/systemd/system# systemctl status elasticsearch
● elasticsearch.service - Elasticsearch
   Loaded: loaded (/lib/systemd/system/elasticsearch.service; enabled; vendor preset: enabled)
   Active: active (running) since Sat 2019-08-31 14:11:24 UTC; 24min ago
     Docs: http://www.elastic.co
 Main PID: 5010 (java)
    Tasks: 50 (limit: 4642)
   Memory: 1.2G
   CGroup: /system.slice/elasticsearch.service
           ├─5010 /usr/share/elasticsearch/jdk/bin/java -Xms1g -Xmx1g -XX:+UseConcMarkSweepGC -X
           └─5122 /usr/share/elasticsearch/modules/x-pack-ml/platform/linux-x86_64/bin/controlle

Aug 31 14:11:24 iwcdev systemd[1]: Started Elasticsearch.
Aug 31 14:11:25 iwcdev elasticsearch[5010]: OpenJDK 64-Bit Server VM warning: Option UseConcMark
Aug 31 14:11:43 iwcdev systemd[1]: elasticsearch.service: Current command vanished from the unit
```

Install Open JDK

1. **Run** the following command to make sure your repository package lists are up to date:

   apt-get update -y

   ```
   root@iwcdev:/lib/systemd/system# apt-get update -y
   Hit:1 http://es.archive.ubuntu.com/ubuntu disco InRelease
   Get:2 http://es.archive.ubuntu.com/ubuntu disco-updates InRelease [97.5 kB]
   Hit:3 https://artifacts.elastic.co/packages/7.x/apt stable InRelease
   Get:4 http://es.archive.ubuntu.com/ubuntu disco-backports InRelease [88.8 kB]
   Get:5 http://es.archive.ubuntu.com/ubuntu disco-security InRelease [97.5 kB]
   Reading package lists... Done
   E: Release file for http://es.archive.ubuntu.com/ubuntu/dists/disco-updates/InRelease is not vali
   d yet (invalid for another 30min 34s). Updates for this repository will not be applied.
   E: Release file for http://es.archive.ubuntu.com/ubuntu/dists/disco-backports/InRelease is not va
   lid yet (invalid for another 30min 56s). Updates for this repository will not be applied.
   E: Release file for http://es.archive.ubuntu.com/ubuntu/dists/disco-security/InRelease is not val
   id yet (invalid for another 30min 20s). Updates for this repository will not be applied.
   ```

2. **Run** the following command to install openjdk-11-jdk:

   apt install openjdk-8-jdk

   ```
   root@iwcdev:/lib/systemd/system# apt install openjdk-8-jdk
   Reading package lists... Done
   Building dependency tree
   Reading state information... Done
   The following additional packages will be installed:
     ca-certificates-java fonts-dejavu-extra java-common libatk-wrapper-java
     libatk-wrapper-java-jni libgail-common libgail18 libgtk2.0-0 libgtk2.0-bin libgtk2.0-common
     libice-dev libpthread-stubs0-dev libsm-dev libx11-dev libxau-dev libxcb1-dev libxdmcp-dev
     libxt-dev openjdk-8-jdk-headless openjdk-8-jre openjdk-8-jre-headless x11proto-core-dev
     x11proto-dev xorg-sgml-doctools xtrans-dev
   ```

3. **Run** the following command to ensure you have correctly installed openjdk:

   java -version

   ```
   root@iwcdev:/lib/systemd/system# java -version
   openjdk version "1.8.0_222"
   OpenJDK Runtime Environment (build 1.8.0_222-8u222-b10-1ubuntu1~19.04.1-b10)
   OpenJDK 64-Bit Server VM (build 25.222-b10, mixed mode)
   root@iwcdev:/lib/systemd/system#
   ```

Install Logstash

Before installing Logstash you need to make sure you have a version of Java 8, 11, or OpenJDK. In the previous steps we installed OpenJDK to meet these requirements. You always want to make sure that your Advanced Packaging Tool (APT) is up to date with the current Elastic repository listing, but we already did that at the beginning of this walk through for Elasticsearch. If you decide that you want to user other Elastic addons later, you can only use the current version that matches your Elasticsearch build.

The APT is a utility used in terminal — as we discussed earlier — to manage software for Debian based Linux distributions for using dpkg packing system. Likewise, it works with core libraries to facilitate the installation and removal of software.

1. **Run** the following command to install logstash:

   sudo apt-get update && sudo apt-get install logstash

```
iwcdev@iwcdev:~/Downloads$ sudo apt-get update && sudo apt-get install logstash
Hit:1 http://es.archive.ubuntu.com/ubuntu disco InRelease
Hit:2 https://artifacts.elastic.co/packages/7.x/apt stable InRelease
Get:3 http://es.archive.ubuntu.com/ubuntu disco-updates InRelease [97.5 kB]
Get:4 http://es.archive.ubuntu.com/ubuntu disco-backports InRelease [88.8 kB]
Get:5 http://es.archive.ubuntu.com/ubuntu disco-security InRelease [97.5 kB]
Get:6 http://es.archive.ubuntu.com/ubuntu disco-updates/universe amd64 Packages [295 kB]
Fetched 295 kB in 1s (275 kB/s)
Reading package lists... Done
Reading package lists... Done
Building dependency tree
```

Starting the Logstash service

1. **Run** the following command to start the logstash service:

   sudo systemctl start logstash.service

   Logstash does not start on its own as a service after installation. Logstash places the system files in the /etc/system/system folder for Debian.

2. **Check** to see that logstash.service is running using the following command:

   systemctl status logstash.service

```
iwcdev@iwcdev:~/Downloads$ systemctl status logstash.service
● logstash.service - logstash
   Loaded: loaded (/etc/systemd/system/logstash.service; disabled; vendor preset: enabled)
   Active: active (running) since Sat 2019-08-31 16:59:57 UTC; 7s ago
 Main PID: 10576 (java)
    Tasks: 14 (limit: 4642)
   Memory: 391.3M
   CGroup: /system.slice/logstash.service
           └─10576 /bin/java -Xms1g -Xmx1g -XX:+UseConcMarkSweepGC -XX:CMSInitiatingOccupancyF

Aug 31 16:59:57 iwcdev systemd[1]: Started logstash.
lines 1-10/10 (END)
```

3. **Run** the following command to change directory to /usr/share/logstash:

   cd /usr/share/logstash

4. **Run** the following to stop logstash services:

   systemctl stop logstash

5. **Run** the following command to set the path for logstash and start Logstash:

   sudo bin/logstash -f /etc/logstash/conf.d/ --path.settings /etc/logstash/

```
iwcdev@iwcdev:/usr/share/logstash$ sudo bin/logstash -f /etc/logstash/conf.d/ --
path.settings /etc/logstash/
Thread.exclusive is deprecated, use Thread::Mutex
Sending Logstash logs to /var/log/logstash which is now configured via log4j2.pr
operties
[2019-10-16T19:56:53,592][WARN ][logstash.config.source.multilocal] Ignoring the
 'pipelines.yml' file because modules or command line options are specified
[2019-10-16T19:56:53,600][INFO ][logstash.runner          ] Starting Logstash {"
logstash.version"=>"7.4.0"}
[2019-10-16T19:56:54,073][INFO ][logstash.config.source.local.configpathloader]
No config files found in path {:path=>"/etc/logstash/conf.d/*"}
[2019-10-16T19:56:54,078][ERROR][logstash.config.sourceloader] No configuration
found in the configured sources.
[2019-10-16T19:56:54,317][INFO ][logstash.agent           ] Successfully started
 Logstash API endpoint {:port=>9600}
[2019-10-16T19:56:59,414][INFO ][logstash.runner          ] Logstash shut down.
```

> *Note: The reason we started Logstash was to ensure it installed correctly. After starting the service, we stopped the service so that we could restart Logstash and set the path.*

Install Kibana

Ensure you are installing the same version of Kibana as your Elasticsearch installation.

1. **Run** the following command to ensure your APT is up to date and subsequently **install** Kibana.

   sudo apt-get update && sudo apt-get install kibana

2. **Run** the following commands to ensure the Kibana service is enabled:

   sudo /bin/systemctl daemon-reload

   sudo /bin/systemctl enable kibana.service

```
iwcdev@iwcdev:~/Downloads$ sudo /bin/systemctl daemon-reload
[sudo] password for iwcdev:
iwcdev@iwcdev:~/Downloads$ sudo /bin/systemctl enable kibana.service
Synchronizing state of kibana.service with SysV service script with /lib/systemd/systemd-sysv-insta
ll.
Executing: /lib/systemd/systemd-sysv-install enable kibana
Created symlink /etc/systemd/system/multi-user.target.wants/kibana.service → /etc/systemd/system/ki
bana.service.
iwcdev@iwcdev:~/Downloads$
```

3. **Run** the following **2** commands to start the kibana.service, and check to make sure it is running:

    sudo systemctl start kibana.service

    sudo systemctl status kibana.service

```
iwcdev@iwcdev:~/Downloads$ sudo systemctl start kibana.service
iwcdev@iwcdev:~/Downloads$ sudo systemctl status kibana.service
● kibana.service - Kibana
   Loaded: loaded (/etc/systemd/system/kibana.service; enabled; vendor preset: enabled)
   Active: active (running) since Sat 2019-08-31 17:40:18 UTC; 10s ago
 Main PID: 19840 (node)
    Tasks: 11 (limit: 4642)
   Memory: 374.0M
   CGroup: /system.slice/kibana.service
           └─19840 /usr/share/kibana/bin/../node/bin/node --no-warnings --max-http-header-size=6553

Aug 31 17:40:18 iwcdev systemd[1]: Started Kibana.
Aug 31 17:40:19 iwcdev kibana[19840]: {"type":"log","@timestamp":"2019-08-31T17:40:19Z","tags":["in
Aug 31 17:40:19 iwcdev kibana[19840]: {"type":"log","@timestamp":"2019-08-31T17:40:19Z","tags":["in
Aug 31 17:40:19 iwcdev kibana[19840]: {"type":"log","@timestamp":"2019-08-31T17:40:19Z","tags":["in
lines 1-13/13 (END)
```

Install Filebeat

1. **Run** the following command:

    sudo apt-get install filebeat -y

```
iwcdev@iwcdev:~$ sudo apt-get install filebeat
[sudo] password for iwcdev:
Reading package lists... Done
Building dependency tree
Reading state information... Done
The following NEW packages will be installed:
  filebeat
```

2. **Run** the following command to configure Filebeat to run on startup:

    sudo update-rc.d filebeat defaults 95 10

Post Install Configuration

After installing the apps, we are going to need to configure them to work together. The website for

Kibana Configuration

1. **Run** the following command to **Change Directory** into the /etc/kibana folder:

   cd /etc/kibana

2. **Run** the following command to switch to Super User and **enter** your SU password:

   sudo su

3. **Run** the following command to edit your kibana.yml:

   nano kibana.yml

4. **Edit** your kibana.yml file to look as follows (un-hash, or add the following lines):

   server.port: 5601
   server.host: "localhost"
   elasticsearch.host: [localhost:9200]

```
# Kibana is served by a back end server. This setting specifies the port to use.
server.port: 5601

# Specifies the address to which the Kibana server will bind. IP addresses and ho$
# The default is 'localhost', which usually means remote machines will not be abl$
# To allow connections from remote users, set this parameter to a non-loopback ad$
server.host: "localhost"

# Enables you to specify a path to mount Kibana at if you are running behind a pr$
# Use the `server.rewriteBasePath` setting to tell Kibana if it should remove the$
# from requests it receives, and to prevent a deprecation warning at startup.
# This setting cannot end in a slash.
#server.basePath: ""

# Specifies whether Kibana should rewrite requests that are prefixed with
# `server.basePath` or require that they are rewritten by your reverse proxy.
# This setting was effectively always `false` before Kibana 6.3 and will
# default to `true` starting in Kibana 7.0.
#server.rewriteBasePath: false

# The maximum payload size in bytes for incoming server requests.
#server.maxPayloadBytes: 1048576

# The Kibana server's name.  This is used for display purposes.
#server.name: "your-hostname"

# The URLs of the Elasticsearch instances to use for all your queries.
elasticsearch.hosts: ["http://localhost:9200"]

# When this setting's value is true Kibana uses the hostname specified in the ser$
```

5. **Run** the following commands to save, and exit the file:

   press "ctrl and X"

   press "Y"

   NOTE: DO NOT CHANGE THE FILE NAME

   press "Return"

Elasticsearch Configuration

2. **Run** the following command to change directory to /etc/elasticsearch:

   cd /etc/elasticsearch

3. **Run** the following command to edit the elastisticsearch.yml:

   nano elasticsearch.yml

4. Ensure the following commands are un-hashed within your elasticsearch.yml:

   path.data: /var/lib/elasticsearch

   path.logs: /var/log/elasticsearch

   network.host: localhost

   http.port: 9200

Note: There is a lot of data within the elasticsearch.yml file, and it is hashed out just like the Kibana file. In my setup the whole file is hashed out besides the information above. See the example below.

```
# -------------------------------- Paths --------------------------------------
#
# Path to directory where to store the data (separate multiple locations by comma$
#
path.data: /var/lib/elasticsearch
#
# Path to log files:
#
path.logs: /var/log/elasticsearch
#
# -------------------------------- Memory --------------------------------------
#
# Lock the memory on startup:
#
#bootstrap.memory_lock: true
#
# Make sure that the heap size is set to about half the memory available
# on the system and that the owner of the process is allowed to use this
# limit.
#
# Elasticsearch performs poorly when the system is swapping the memory.
#
# -------------------------------- Network --------------------------------------
#
# Set the bind address to a specific IP (IPv4 or IPv6):
#
network.host: localhost
#
# Set a custom port for HTTP:
#
http.port: 9200
```

5. **Run** the following commands to save, and exit the file:

    press "ctrl and X"

    press "Y"

    NOTE: DO NOT CHANGE THE FILE NAME.

    press "Return"

Enter your password if required. It did not require me to enter my password because I was already SU.

Filebeat Configuration

1. **Run** the following command to change directory to /etc/filebeat/

   cd /etc/filebeat/

2. **Run** the following command to enable Filebeat:

   systemctl enable filebeat

```
root@iwcdev:/etc/filebeat# systemctl enable filebeat
Synchronizing state of filebeat.service with SysV service script with /lib/systemd/syste
md-sysv-install.
Executing: /lib/systemd/systemd-sysv-install enable filebeat
root@iwcdev:/etc/filebeat#
```

3. **Run** the following command to edit the filebeat.yml:

   nano filebeat.yml

4. **Input** the following settings into the filebeat.yml file but ensure that you follow the correct syntax when entering the information. Your Zeek (Bro) path needs to be set to where your Zeek (Bro) logs are located; the path we used earlier doing the PF_RING, and Zeek (Bro) IDS installation and configuration. Remember that YML is sensitive to formatting errors and it has to have the correct spacing:

```
filebeat.inputs:

- type: log
  enabled: false
  paths:
   - /opt/zeek/logs/current/*.log


name: zeek-beat


tags: ["zeek"]


filebeat.config.modules:

 path: ${path.config}/modules.d/*.yml


setup.kibana:


setup.dashboards.enabled: true
setup.dashboards.directory: ${path.home}/kibana
setup.dashboards.beat: filebeat


output.elasticsearch:


 hosts: ["localhost:9200"]
```

> *Note: Pay attention to the spacing, if the filebeat index isn't working correctly in kibana, it could be due to spacing issues. Refer to the filebeat.reference.yml file within the /etc/filebeat folder for a look at the example settings, and the syntax for each*

```
#################### Filebeat Configuration Example ####################
#======================= Filebeat inputs ==============
filebeat.inputs:
# Each - is an input. Most options can be set at the input level, so
# you can use different inputs for various configurations.
# Below are the input specific configurations.
- type: log
    # Change to true to enable this input configuration.
  enabled: false
    # Paths that should be crawled and fetched. Glob based paths.
  paths:
    - /opt/zeek/logs/current/*.log
    #===================== General ==============
    # The name of the shipper that publishes the network data. It can be used to
    # all the transactions sent by a single shipper in the web interface.
name: zeek-beat
    # The tags of the shipper are included in their own field with each
    # transaction published.
tags: ["zeek"]
    # Optional fields that you can specify to add additional information to the
    # output.
    #fields:
    #  env: staging
filebeat.config.modules:
  path: ${path.config}/modules.d/*.yml
    #may need to remove the kibana line not sure...
setup.kibana:
  host: "localhost:5601"
setup.dashboards.enabled: true
setup.dashboards.directory: ${path.home}/kibana
setup.dashboards.beat: filebeat


#===================== Outputs ==============
    #------------------- Logstash output -----
output.elasticsearch:
      # The Logstash hosts
  hosts: ["localhost:9200"]
#  pipeline: geoip-info
      # Optional SSL. By default is off.
      # List of root certificates for HTTPS server verifications
      #ssl.certificate_authorities: ["/etc/pki/root/ca.pem"]
      # Certificate for SSL client authentication
      #ssl.certificate: "/etc/filebeat/ssl/logstash.crt"
      # Client Certificate Key
      #ssl.key: "/etc/pki/client/cert.key"
```

Note: The update from 7.3.1 to 7.4 changed a few things in the filebeat.yml file; it contains some things 7.3.1 did not have. For people using the new version this is a good thing because it takes away a lot of the research needed to set up Filebeat from scratch. I would manually adjust the file to contain the information I have loaded. I tried to copy and paste it directly, and sometimes it works and other times it doesn't. This happens sometimes even on a mirrored install I used to check the walk-through on. For anyone that's used open source software they will be familiar with these issues. With that being said, double check everything if you're having issues.

5. **Run** the following command to change to the modules.d directory:

cd modules.d

If you run the ls (list) command in the module.d folder you can see all the modules that are available for Filebeat.

```
root@iwcdev:/etc/filebeat/modules.d# ls
apache.yml.disabled         iptables.yml.disabled   osquery.yml.d:
auditd.yml.disabled         kafka.yml.disabled      panw.yml.disat
cisco.yml.disabled          kibana.yml.disabled     postgresql.yml
coredns.yml.disabled        logstash.yml.disabled   rabbitmq.yml.d
elasticsearch.yml.disabled  mongodb.yml.disabled    redis.yml.disa
envoyproxy.yml.disabled     mssql.yml.disabled      santa.yml.disa
googlecloud.yml.disabled    mysql.yml.disabled      suricata.yml.d
haproxy.yml.disabled        nats.yml.disabled       system.yml.disabled
icinga.yml.disabled         netflow.yml.disabled    traefik.yml.disabled
iis.yml.disabled            nginx.yml.disabled      zeek.yml.disabled
root@iwcdev:/etc/filebeat/modules.d# 
```

6. **Run** the following command to enable the Zeek (Bro) module:

filebeat modules enable zeek

7. **Run** the following command to edit the zeek.yml:

nano zeek.yml

8. **Input** the following information:

- module: zeek

connection:

enabled: true

var.paths: ["/opt/zeek/logs/current/conn.log"]

dns:

enabled: true

var.paths: ["/opt/zeek/logs/current/dns.log"]

http:

enabled: true

var.paths: ["/opt/zeek/logs/current/http.log"]

files:

  enabled: true

  var.paths: ["/opt/zeek/logs/current/files.log"]

ssl:

  enabled: true

  var.paths: ["/opt/zeek/logs/current/ssl.log"]

notice:

  enabled: true

  var.paths: ["/opt/zeek/logs/current/notice.log"]

Run the following commands to save, and exit the file:

press "ctrl and X" and press "Y"

NOTE: DO NOT CHANGE THE FILE NAME.

press "Return"

```
Module: zeek
# Docs: https://www.elastic.co/guide/en/beats/filebeat/7.3/f

- module: zeek
  # All logs
  connection:
    enabled: true
    var.paths: ["/opt/zeek/logs/current/conn.log"]
  dns:
    enabled: true
    var.paths: ["/opt/zeek/logs/current/dns.log"]
  http:
    enabled: true
    var.paths: ["/opt/zeek/logs/current/http.log"]
  files:
    enabled: true
    var.paths: ["/opt/zeek/logs/current/files.log"]
  ssl:
    enabled: true
    var.paths: ["/opt/zeek/logs/current/ssl.log"]
  notice:
    enabled: true
    var.paths: ["/opt/zeek/logs/current/notice.log"]
    # Set custom paths for the log files. If left empty,
    # Filebeat will choose the paths depending on your OS.
    #var.paths:
```

Note: You need to put the path to your Zeek (Bro) logs and if you do not want to view or monitor a specific type of log you can set the enabled command to false.

Zeek (Bro) Configuration

1. **Run** the following command to go to the directory used to edit the output for Zeek (Bro) to configure it to use JSON:

   cd /opt/zeek/share/zeek/base/frameworks/logging/writers

2. **Run** the following command to edit the ascii.zeek file:

   nano ascii.zeek

3. **Edit** the following line:

   This may already be set, if so disregard, but if it has an F, then change it to T.

   const use_json = T &redef;

```
module LogAscii;

export {
        ## If true, output everything to stdout rather than
        ## into files. This is primarily for debugging purposes.
        ##
        ## This option is also available as a per-filter ``$config`` option.
        const output_to_stdout = F &redef;

        ## If true, the default will be to write logs in a JSON format.
        ##
        ## This option is also available as a per-filter ``$config`` option.
        const use_json = T &redef;
```

4. **Run** the following commands to save, and exit the file:

   press "ctrl and X"

   press "Y"

   NOTE: DO NOT CHANGE THE FILE NAME.

press "Return"

5. **Run** the following command to change directory to the site folder, ensure you use your $PREFIX/share/zeek/site/:

cd /opt/zeek/share/zeek/site

My prefix is /opt/zeek for my zeek folder.

6. **Run** the following command to edit the local.zeek file to enable JSON output:

nano local.zeek

7. **Input** the following information into the file and replace **@load tuning/defaults** with these lines:

@load tuning/json-logs
redef LogAscii::json_timestamps = JSON: :TS_EPOCH;
redef LogAscii::use_json = T;

Note: Make sure you are using the EPOCH timestamp output if you are not already. This is a lesson I learned the hard way because I thought the module would work with any Zeek (Bro) output, but the Kibana Module will not be able to parse GeoIP locations without having the time formatted with EPOCH. Like I stated before, Elastic is sensitive to having the correct settings.

Before

```
# This script logs which scripts were loaded during each run.
@load misc/loaded-scripts

# Apply the default tuning scripts for common tuning settings.
@load tuning/defaults

# Estimate and log capture loss.
@load misc/capture-loss

# Enable logging of memory, packet and lag statistics.
@load misc/stats
```

After:

```
##! Local site policy. Customize as appropriate.
##!
##! This file will not be overwritten when upgrading or reinstalling!

# This script logs which scripts were loaded during each run.
@load misc/loaded-scripts

# Apply the default tuning scripts for common tuning settings.
#@load tuning/defaults  ##ADDED THE FOLLOWING 3 LINES
@load tuning/json-logs
redef LogAscii::json_timestamps = JSON::TS_EPOCH;
redef LogAscii::use_json = T;
# Estimate and log capture loss.
@load misc/capture-loss

# Enable logging of memory, packet and lag statistics.
@load misc/stats
```

8. **Run** the following commands to save, and exit the file:

   press "ctrl and X"

   press "Y"

   NOTE: DO NOT CHANGE THE FILE NAME.

   press "Return"

Using ELK Stack with Zeek (Bro) IDS

Before we start, we need to ensure that all of the services are currently running. Also, ensure that Zeek (Bro) is running and generating logs.

Refer to the Zeek (Bro) installation to start up Zeek (Bro) if you haven't already done so.

1. **Run** the following commands to restart all of the services for Elasticsearch, Kibana, and Filebeat to ensure all of our changes took effect:

   systemctl restart elasticsearch
   systemctl restart kibana
   systemctl restart filebeat

2. **Run** the following commands to see if the services are working:

   systemctl status filebeat
   systemctl status elasticsearch
   systemctl status kibana

Note: You should see an output similar to the picture below for all three services, but you need to ensure it says active like it shows below. If it does not, read the parse error and/or go to /var/log/filebeat/filebeat.log, or the /var/log/message log and see what the log says. These files are really sensitive — if there are any extra spaces or if anything is out of place — the program will fail. I just want to note that some areas of the files use quotes, the type of quote can cause it to fail — like using dual quotes, but not single and vice versa. Also, some places you can remove quotes all together. I have not found a reason that I can identify that causes this, because I've literally had to do it different ways after walking through this install multiple times and even repeating the steps.

```
root@iwcdev:/etc/filebeat# systemctl status filebeat
● filebeat.service - Filebeat sends log files to Logstash or dir
    Loaded: loaded (/lib/systemd/system/filebeat.service; enabled
    Active: active (running) since Mon 2019-10-07 22:31:27 EDT; 3
      Docs: https://www.elastic.co/products/beats/filebeat
  Main PID: 7411 (filebeat)
```

The following picture shows what it will look like if the service has failed. These modules fail sometimes for many reasons, always check the statuses and restart them if they are failed.

```
● filebeat.service - Filebeat sends log files to
    Loaded: loaded (/lib/systemd/system/filebeat.s
    Active: failed (Result: exit-code) since Mon 2
      Docs: https://www.elastic.co/products/beats/
  Main PID: 7137 (code=exited, status=1/FAILURE)
```

3. To **view** Kibana, open your web browser and **enter** to the following address:

127.0.0.1:5601

or

localhost:5601

You will then be redirected to the main page of Kibana.

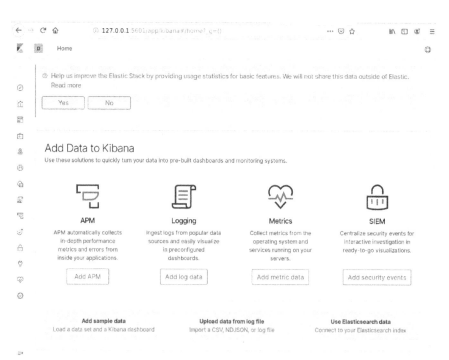

4. **Click** the **discover** icon on the top left of the Kibana page:

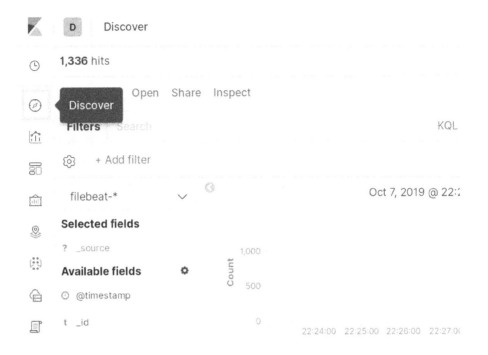

5. **Click** the **Default** icon in the top left:

6. **Click** the **Manage spaces** link:

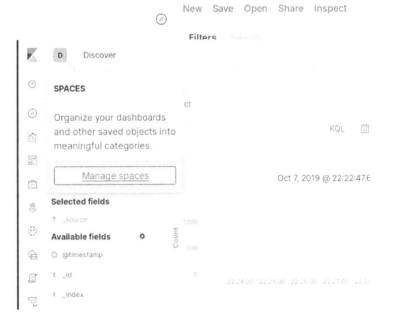

7. **Click** the **Index Patterns** icon:

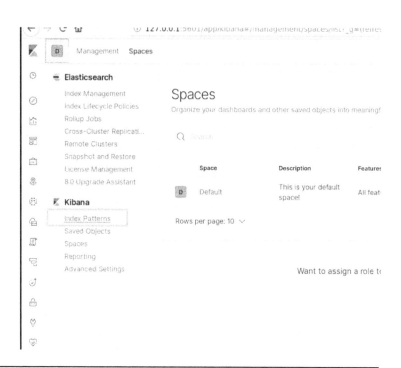

> *Note: You need to run Zeek (Bro) so that it generates logs for this part to work. Notice, I have 3 different sets of logs there from different days. This was because I have already configured the module during the write up and ran Zeek (Bro) to send logs to Elasticsearch via Filebeat.*

8. **Click** the **Create index pattern** icon:

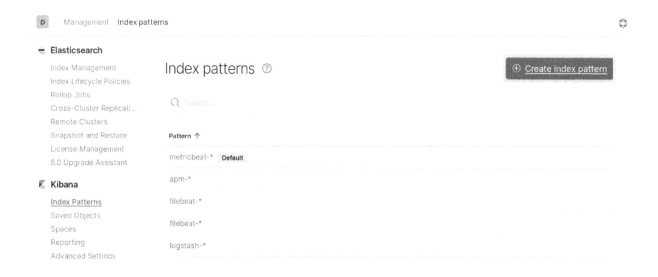

9. **Type** filebeat-* and **click** the **Next Step** icon (If Fillebeat is already there, just move on to the Zeek (Bro) configuration steps next):

> *Note: Ensure you use filebeat-* or the Zeek (Bro) module will not know where to pull data from.*

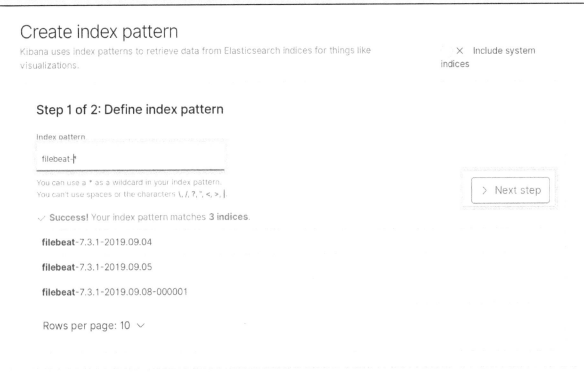

10. **Select @timestamp** from the drop down, and **click Create index pattern**:

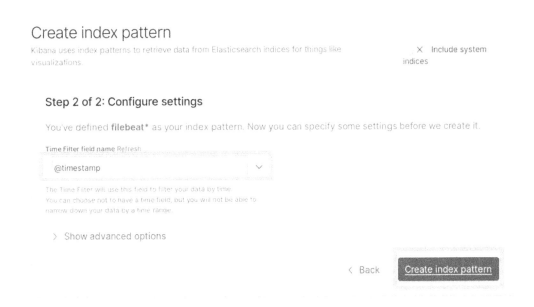

11. **Click** the **Refresh** icon so that all the fields coming in from Zeek (Bro) are properly identified in Kibana.

filebeat*

Time Filter field name: @timestamp

This page lists every field in the **filebeat*** index and the field's associated core type as recorded by Elasticsearch. To change a field type, use the Elasticsearch Mapping API %

Fields (1043)   Scripted fields (0)   Source filters (0)

Q Filter   All field types

Name	Type	Format	Searchable	Aggregatable	Excluded
@timestamp ⏱	date		●	●	
@version	string		●		
@version.keyword	string		●	●	
_id	string		●	●	
_index	string		●	●	

Note: You can always go back and do this if there are exclamation point icons showing by the fields when viewing the log entry in the Discover section of Kibana.

Configuring the Zeek Overview Dashboard

1. Go back to discover by **clicking** the **discover** icon:

The picture above shows the logs that are now being generated.

2. **Click** on the **dashboard** icon and then **click** the
   Zeek (Bro) Overview Dashboard link:

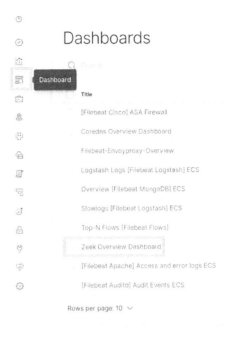

You should now see an output similar to the following image. Please note, the logs need to generate over time before everything will populate into the dashboard. I've been running logs randomly throughout this process, so everything has had time to populate here. Give your logs some time, and if they do not show eventually, check all the configuration files to ensure you have everything precisely how this walk through shows it.

This concludes the installation of Elasticsearch, Kibana, Logstash, and Filebeat along with configuration for using the Zeek (Bro) module to ingest logs to Elasticsearch and view them in the Zeek (Bro) Dashboard. The next part of this walk-through will go over how to use Logstash to ingest logs from Filebeat and configure the beats to view the logs within Elasticsearch and Kibana.

The method of ingesting logs from Logstash into Elasticsearch and viewing them in Kibana is how the ELK stack got its name. The other method above was for people who do not need to use Logstash. Logstash is very powerful and can pull logs from many different applications across a vast network from many different nodes. The next part of this walk through shows how to setup Logstash, Filebeat, and Zeek (Bro) to ingest data from Zeek (Bro) and send it through the Logstash pipeline to Elasticsearch.

Alternative ELK Stack Method

Configure Zeek (Bro) to Use JSON Output

> *Note: Some of the configuration files we used in the walk through earlier are not the same for this. Furthermore, you will need to change the files to match the following steps. Ensure you perform the steps in the previous configuration with the exception of*

/opt/zeek/share/zeek/base/frameworks/logging/writers/ascii.zeek

/opt/zeek/share/zeek/site/local.zeek

/etc/filebeat/filbeat.yml

/etc/logstash/conf.d/zeek.conf

/etc/logstash/pipelines.yml

/etc/logstash/logstash.yml

/etc/filebeat/modules/zeek.yml

1. **Run** the following command to switch to Super User and enter your su password:

   sudo su

2. **Change directory** to the **/opt/zeek/share/zeek/**site by using the following command in terminal:

   cd /opt/zeek/share/zeek/site

3. **Run** the following command to edit the **local.zeek** file:

   nano local.zeek

4. **Input** the following information for turning on JSON output with the TS_ISO8601 timestamp output:

@load tuning/json-logs

redef LogAscii::json_timestamps = JSON::TS_ISO8601;

redef LogAscii::use_json = T;

It is important you use this timestamp output, because of the index template used with Logstash in Elasticsearch

```
 Q                    root@iwcdev: /opt/zeek/share/zeek/site
  GNU nano 3.2                         local.zeek
##! Local site policy. Customize as appropriate.
##!
##! This file will not be overwritten when upgrading or reinstalling!

# This script logs which scripts were loaded during each run.
@load misc/loaded-scripts

# Apply the default tuning scripts for common tuning settings.
#@load tuning/defaults   ##ADDED THE FOLLOWING 3 LINES
@load tuning/json-logs
redef LogAscii::json_timestamps = JSON::TS_ISO8601;
redef LogAscii::use_json = T;
```

5. **Run** the following commands to save, and exit the file:

press "ctrl and X"

press "Y"

NOTE: DO NOT CHANGE THE FILE NAME.

press "Return"

6. **Change directory** into the /opt/zeek/share/zeek/base/frameworks/logging/writers directory by running the following command:

cd /opt/zeek/share/zeek/base/frameworks/logging/writers

7. **Run** the following command to edit the **ascii.zeek** file:

nano ascii.zeek

8. **Edit** the **ascii.zeek** file to ensure the following line has the json output set to **T** for True:

const use_json = T &redef;

```
module LogAscii;

export {
        ## If true, output everything to stdout rather than
        ## into files. This is primarily for debugging purposes.
        ##
        ## This option is also available as a per-filter ``$config`` option.
        const output_to_stdout = F &redef;

        ## If true, the default will be to write logs in a JSON format.
        ##
        ## This option is also available as a per-filter ``$config`` option.
        const use_json = T &redef;

        ## If true, valid UTF-8 sequences will pass through unescaped and be
        ## written into logs.
        ##
        ## This option is also available as a per-filter ``$config`` option.
        const enable_utf_8 = F &redef;

        ## Define the gzip level to compress the logs.  If 0, then no gzip
```

9. **Run** the following commands to save, and exit the file:

press "ctrl and X"

press "Y"

NOTE: DO NOT CHANGE THE FILE NAME.

press "Return"

Configure Logstash

1. **Change directory** to the **/etc/logstash** directory:

cd /etc/logstash

2. **Run** the following command to edit the **pipelines.yml** file:

nano pipelines.yml

3. **Edit** the **pipelines.yml** to contain the following information (if it is already configured skip this step):

- pipeline.id: main

  path.config: "/etc/logstash/conf.d/*.conf"

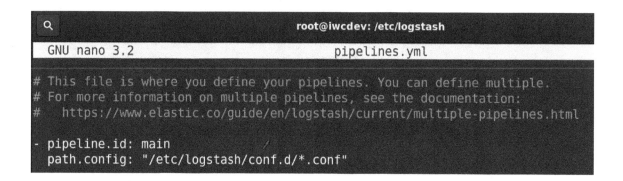

4. **Run** the following command to edit the **logstash.yml**:

> **Note**: This file functions by setting a folder where the pipeline will come from. You can have multiple configuration files in this folder that makes ingesting from multiple sources easier to manage. This folder is the default location used by Logstash. If you use another directory, then set the new directory location path.

nano logstash.yml

5. **Edit** the Logstash file to contain the following information and leave the rest hashed:

path.data: /var/lib/logstash
path.logs: /var/log/logstash

```
# ----------- Data path ----------------
#
# Which directory should be used by logstash and its plugins
# for any persistent needs. Defaults to LOGSTASH_HOME/data
#
path.data: /var/lib/logstash
#
# ----------- Pipeline Settings --------------
```

```
# ----------- Debugging Settings --------------
#
# Options for log.level:
#   * fatal
#   * error
#   * warn
#   * info (default)
#   * debug
#   * trace
#
# log.level: info
path.logs: /var/log/logstash
#
```

Note: This should already be configured, if not it's in the default file, just un-hash it.

6. **Run** the following commands to save, and exit the file:

   press "ctrl and X"
   press "Y"

   NOTE: DO NOT CHANGE THE FILE NAME.

   press "Return"

7. **Change directory** to the /etc/logstash/conf.d folder:

   cd conf.d

8. **Run** the following command to create and edit the zeek.conf file:

nano zeek.conf

9. **Paste** the following information into the zeek.conf file:

```
input {
  beats {
    port => 5001
    codec => "json"
#    ssl => true
#    ssl_certificate =>
"/etc/logstash/logstash.crt"
#    ssl_key => "/etc/logstash/logstash.key"
  }
}


filter {

  #Let's get rid of those header lines; they begin with a hash
  if [message] =~ /^#/ {
   drop {}
  }


    #Let's convert our timestamp into the 'ts' field, so we can use Kibana features
natively
    date {
     match => [ "ts", "UNIX" ]
    }


    # add geoip attributes
    geoip {
```

Any file in this folder is executed on Logstash's startup; this is where the pipeline files reside.

```
  source => "id.orig_h"
 target => "geoip"
}
geoip {
 source => "id.resp_h"
 target => "geoip"
}
geoip {
 source => "id.resp_h"
 target => "resp_geoip"
}
geoip {
 source => "id.orig_h"
 target => "orig_geoip"
}
```

```
#The following makes use of the translate filter (logstash contrib) to convert
conn_state into human text. Saves having to look up values for packet
introspection
  translate {
   field => "conn_state"

   destination => "conn_state_full"

   dictionary => [
         "S0", "Connection attempt seen, no reply",
         "S1", "Connection established, not terminated",
         "S2", "Connection established and close attempt by originator seen (but
no reply from responder)",
         "S3", "Connection established and close attempt by responder seen (but
no reply from originator)",
         "SF", "Normal SYN/FIN completion",
         "REJ", "Connection attempt rejected",
         "RSTO", "Connection established, originator aborted (sent a RST)",
         "RSTR", "Established, responder aborted",
         "RSTOS0", "Originator sent a SYN followed by a RST, we never saw a
SYN-ACK from the responder",
         "RSTRH", "Responder sent a SYN ACK followed by a RST, we never saw
a SYN from the (purported) originator",
         "SH", "Originator sent a SYN followed by a FIN, we never saw a SYN
ACK from the responder (hence the connection was 'half' open)",
              "SHR", "Responder sent a SYN ACK followed by a FIN, we never
saw a SYN from the originator",
         "OTH", "No SYN seen, just midstream traffic (a 'partial connection' that
was not later closed)"
         ]
```

```
    }
  mutate {
    convert => [ "id.orig_p", "integer" ]
    convert => [ "id.resp_p", "integer" ]
    convert => [ "orig_bytes", "integer" ]
    convert => [ "duration", "float" ]
    convert => [ "resp_bytes", "integer" ]
    convert => [ "missed_bytes", "integer" ]
    convert => [ "orig_pkts", "integer" ]
    convert => [ "orig_ip_bytes", "integer" ]
    convert => [ "resp_pkts", "integer" ]
    convert => [ "resp_ip_bytes", "integer" ]
    rename => [ "id.orig_h", "id_orig_host" ]
    rename => [ "id.orig_p", "id_orig_port" ]
    rename => [ "id.resp_h", "id_resp_host" ]
    rename => [ "id.resp_p", "id_resp_port" ]
  }
}

output {
  stdout { codec => rubydebug }
  elasticsearch {
    hosts => ["localhost:9200"]
    template_overwrite => true
  }
}
```

I have a few extra lines in my output config in the picture below, but you do not need those.

```
input {
    beats {
        port => 5001
        codec => "json"
#       ssl => true
#       ssl_certificate => "/etc/logstash/logstash.crt"
#       ssl_key => "/etc/logstash/logstash.key"
    }
}

filter {

  #Let's get rid of those header lines; they begin with a hash
  if [message] =~ /^#/ {
    drop { }
  }

    #Let's convert our timestamp into the 'ts' field, so we can use Kibana feat$
    date {
      match => [ "ts", "UNIX" ]
    }

    # add geoip attributes
    geoip {
      source => "id.orig_h"
#     target => "orig_geoip"
    }
```
```
[ Read 92 lines ]
```
```
    }
    geoip {
      source => "id.resp_h"
#     target => "resp_geoip"
    }
    geoip {
      source => "id.resp_h"
      target => "resp_geoip"
    }
    geoip {
      source => "id.orig_h"
      target => "orig_geoip"
    }
    #The following makes use of the translate filter (logstash contrib) to conv$
    translate {
```
```
      field => "conn_state"

      destination => "conn_state_full"

      dictionary => [
                    "S0", "Connection attempt seen, no reply",
                    "S1", "Connection established, not terminated",
                    "S2", "Connection established and close attempt by originat$
                    "S3", "Connection established and close attempt by responde$
                    "SF", "Normal SYN/FIN completion",
                    "REJ", "Connection attempt rejected",
                    "RSTO", "Connection established, originator aborted (sent a$
                    "RSTR", "Established, responder aborted",
                    "RSTOS0", "Originator sent a SYN followed by a RST, we neve$
```

```
                "RSTRH", "Responder sent a SYN ACK followed by a RST, we ne$
                "SH", "Originator sent a SYN followed by a FIN, we never sa$
                    "SHR", "Responder sent a SYN ACK followed by a $
                "OTH", "No SYN seen, just midstream traffic (a 'partial con$
                ]
    }

    mutate {
        convert => [ "id.orig_p", "integer" ]
        convert => [ "id.resp_p", "integer" ]
        convert => [ "orig_bytes", "integer" ]
        convert => [ "duration", "float" ]
        convert => [ "resp_bytes", "integer" ]
        convert => [ "missed_bytes", "integer" ]
```

```
        convert => [ "missed_bytes", "integer" ]
        convert => [ "orig_pkts", "integer" ]
        convert => [ "orig_ip_bytes", "integer" ]
        convert => [ "resp_pkts", "integer" ]
        convert => [ "resp_ip_bytes", "integer" ]
        rename => [ "id.orig_h", "id_orig_host" ]
        rename => [ "id.orig_p", "id_orig_port" ]
        rename => [ "id.resp_h", "id_resp_host" ]
        rename => [ "id.resp_p", "id_resp_port" ]
    }
}
```

```
output {
    stdout { codec => rubydebug }
    elasticsearch {
        hosts => ["localhost:9200"]
#        index => "logstash-%{+YYYY.MM.DD}"
#        document_type => "zeek"
#        template => "/etc/logstash/zeek.json"
#        template_name => "zeek"
        template_overwrite => true
    }
}
```

10.   **Run** the following commands to save, and exit the file:

press "ctrl and X"

press "Y"

NOTE: DO NOT CHANGE THE FILE NAME.

press "Return"

There are a lot of things going on in this pipeline file and I provided descriptions within the file with hash tags. In the first section we are setting the input to come from port 5001, which is the port that our Filebeat config will be sending logs to Logstash. I have hashed out the SSL settings because we are not using it, but they are there if you need to reference them.

The next section we are filtering out the information that we are receiving and getting rid of the header lines. Furthermore, we are converting the timestamp to the "ts" field for Kibana to use its native features.

The next portion of the file is establishing what fields contain GeoIP information. Likewise, after the GeoIP information is shown we have placed a dictionary to show what the connection state is in readable terms that are easily identifiable. Let us be honest, we all forget things from time to time, and this makes it really easy to understand our output without having to look at a reference elsewhere.

The last two portions of the file contain a mutation for fields to have them convert the information into a style that Elasticsearch can handle, and then rename a few fields to make it easier to read and understand. The final portion of the file is the output. Setting the stdout to the rubydebug codec allows you to debug errors in Elasticsearch a little easier. The host is our Elasticsearch host, and the template is going to be the default template. Prior to the write up I had a specialized config, but Elasticsearch default template will work perfectly with this Zeek.conf file. Likewise, this is why you see the hashed-out template at the end of the file in the picture of my config. Please note that I hashed out the index log format, and this is so that GeoIP can work with a format it understands like filebeat-%, or logstash-%. I had these lines there for other configurations. The great part about using hashes is that it gives you the ability to leave notes, reminders, or other options that you're not currently using. This is commonly done when writing code because it's hard to remember exactly what you did months ago, and you can always reference back to the file and see your thought process, or other configuration changes you made.

Configure Filebeat

1. **Change directory** to the **/etc/filebeat/** directory:

   cd /etc/filebeat/

2. **Run** the following command to edit the filebeat.yml:

   nano filebeat.yml

3. **Input** the following information into your **filebeat.yml**:

   filebeat.inputs:

   - type: log
       # Change to true to enable this input configuration.
     enabled: true
       # Paths that should be crawled and fetched. Glob based paths.
     paths:
       - /opt/zeek/logs/current/*.log
     #==================== General =============
     # The name of the shipper that publishes the network data. It can be used to group
     # all the transactions sent by a single shipper in the web interface.
     name: zeek-beat
       # The tags of the shipper are included in their own field with each
       # transaction published.

tags: ["zeek"]

Optional fields that you can specify to add additional information to the

output.

#fields:

env: staging

filebeat.config.modules:

path: ${path.config}/modules.d/*.yml

#may need to remove the kibana line not sure...

setup.kibana:

host: "localhost:5601"

setup.dashboards.enabled: true

setup.dashboards.directory: ${path.home}/kibana

setup.dashboards.beat: filebeat

#==================== Outputs ============

#------------------- Logstash output -----

output.logstash:

The Logstash hosts

hosts: ["localhost:5001"]

4. **Run** the following commands to save, and exit the file:

press "ctrl and X"

press "Y"

NOTE: DO NOT CHANGE THE FILE NAME.

press "Return"

5. **Run** the following command to ensure the config file is correct:

filebeat test config -e

Note: You must be root to perform the config test, and your main concern when viewing the output is to see "Config OK." Your output should be similar to the following:

6. **Run** the following commands to restart all ELK Stack services:

   systemctl restart kibana

   systemctl restart elasticsearch

   systemctl restart filebeat

   systemctl restart logstash

7. **Run** the following commands to ensure all the services are working:

   systemctl status kibana

   systemctl status elasticsearch

   systemctl status filebeat

   systemctl status logstash

For those new to linux, press ctrl+c to get out of the status area results.

Ensure Zeek(Bro) is running in order to perform the following steps

Viewing Logstash GEOIP Information in Kibana

1. **Click** the **Discover** icon:

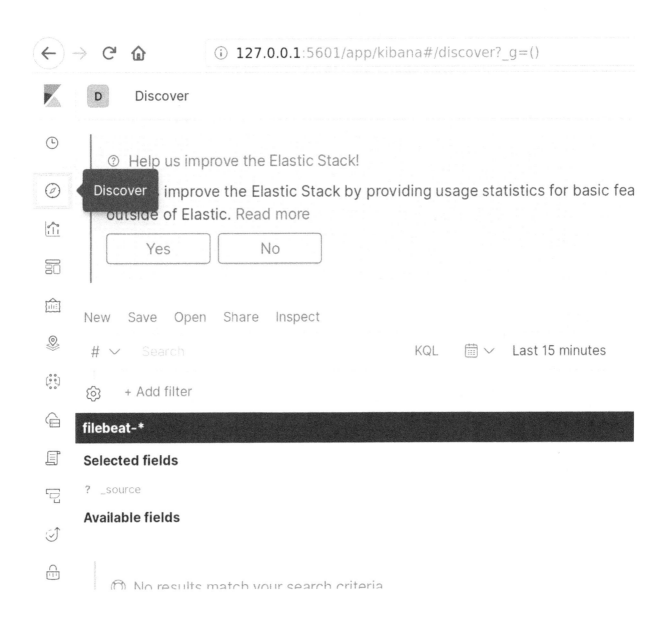

2. **Click** the **Default** icon, and then **click** the **Manage Spaces** link:

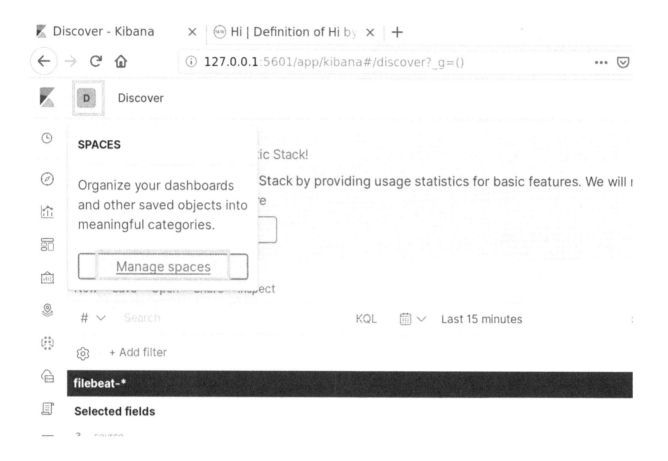

3. **Click** the **Index Patterns** icon and then **click** the **Create index pattern** icon:

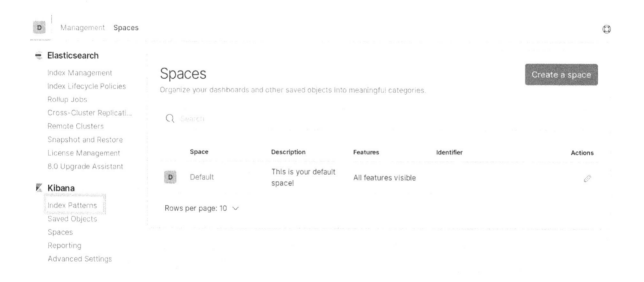

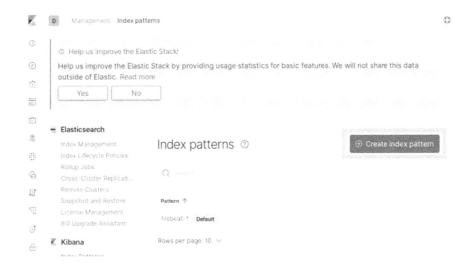

4. Type **logstash-*** into the **index pattern** box and click the **Next step** icon:

Create index pattern

Kibana uses index patterns to retrieve data from Elasticsearch indices for things like visualizations.

✕ Include system indices

Step 1 of 2: Define index pattern

Index pattern

logstash-*

You can use a * as a wildcard in your index pattern.
You can't use spaces or the characters \, /, ?, ", <, >, |.

> Next step

✓ **Success!** Your index pattern matches **1 index**.

logstash-2019.10.17-000001

Rows per page: 10 ∨

5. **Select** the **@timestamp** setting, and **click** the **Create index pattern** icon:

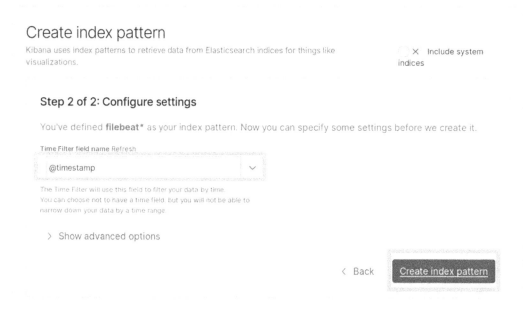

6. **Click** the **visualizations** icon:

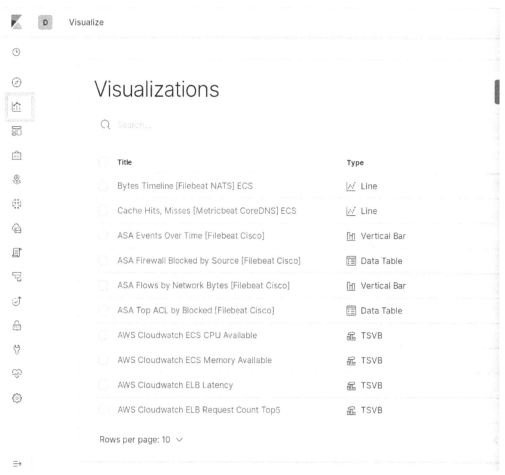

7. **Click** the **create new visualization** icon:

Visualizations

Q map

8. **Click** the **coordinate map** icon:

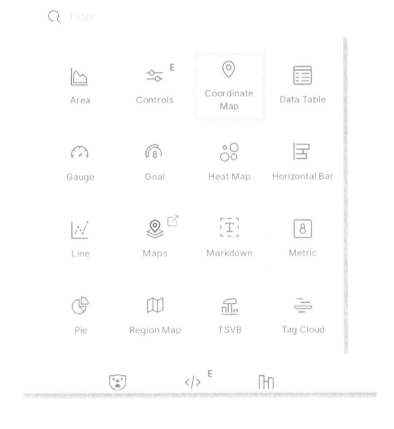

New Visualization

9. **Type** log and **click** logstash-*:

Sort ∨   Types 2 ∨

🔍 log

⬚ logstash-*

○ All ASA Logs [Filebeat Cisco]

10.   **Click** buckets **+ADD**, and **click geo coordinates**:

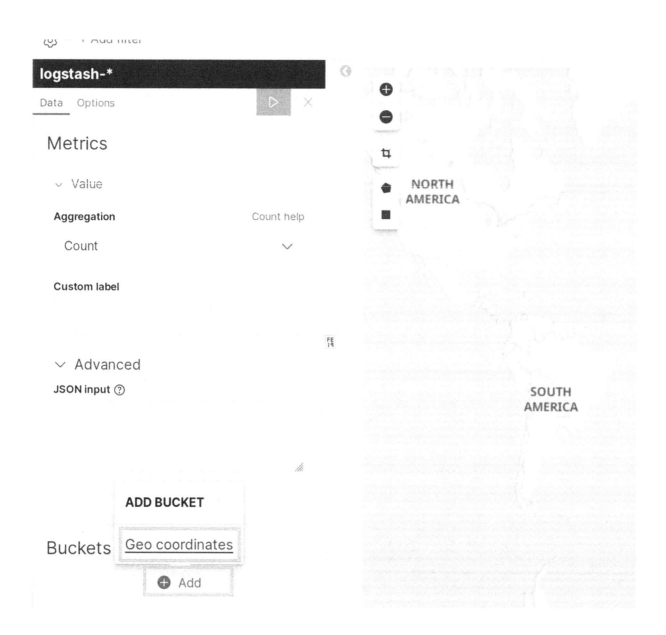

11.   **Select** the **Geohash** selection:

Buckets

Geohash

12. **Select** the **geoip.location** selection:

13. **Click** the **apply changes** icon, and it should pop up on the map.

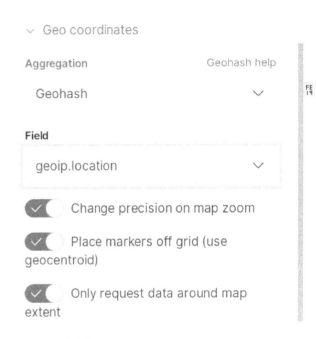

Geo coordinates

Aggregation   Geohash help

Geohash

Field

geoip.location

Change precision on map zoom

Place markers off grid (use geocentroid)

Only request data around map extent

Custom label

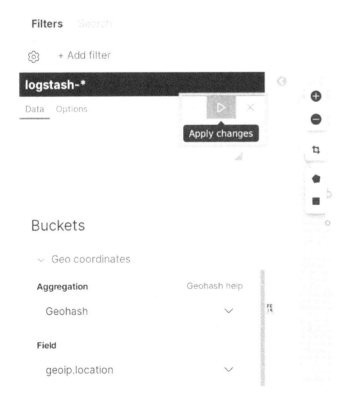

Filters   Search

+ Add filter

logstash-*

Data   Options

Apply changes

Buckets

Geo coordinates

Aggregation   Geohash help

Geohash

Field

geoip.location

After hitting apply changes you should now have a geoip map if you've generated any logs in the selected timeframe.

Troubleshooting Logs in Kibana

If for some reason **Logstash-*** is not showing up in the coordinate map drop downs it is because something has stopped the logs from being recognized by Kibana. Kibana is very sensitive to logs being formatted in correctly and it will not process the data properly to show in the dashboard. Ensure your configurations are correct, and also clear out any old Logstash indexes. While going back through the walk through I had everything exactly the same as my proof source build, and it would not work. After researching this issue I found that I was not the only one. I fixed my issue by deleting any Logstash indexes, and remaking the index pattern.

To remove the Index, and Index pattern perform the following steps:

1. **Click Default.**
2. **Click Index Management.**
3. **Click the Logstash index.**
4. **Click the Manage icon.**
5. **Click Delete index.**

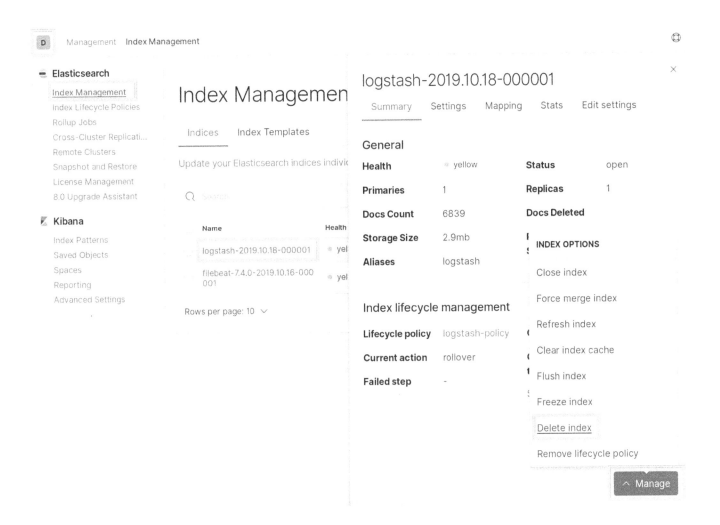

6. **Click** the **Delete index** icon.

Delete index

You are about to delete this index:

• logstash-2019.10.18-000001

You can't recover a deleted index. Make sure you have appropriate backups.

Cancel   Delete index

7. **Click** the **Index Patterns** icon.

8. **Click** the **Logstash-*** index pattern (or whatever name convention is used).

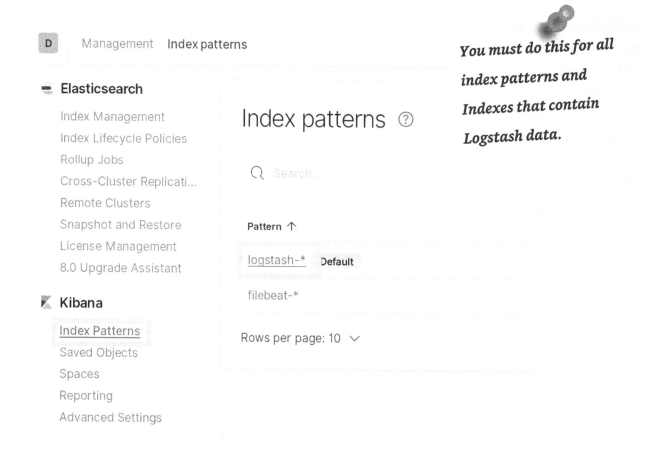

You must do this for all index patterns and Indexes that contain Logstash data.

9. **Click** the **Trashcan** (delete) icon.

★ logstash-*

Time Filter field name: @timestamp   Default

This page lists every field in the **logstash-*** index and the field's associated core type as recorded by Elasticsearch. To change a field type, use the Elasticsearch Mapping API ⚲

Fields (226)   Scripted fields (0)   Source filters (0)

Go back through the steps to restart (systemctl restart) Elasticsearch, Kibana, Filebeat, and Logstash then create the Logstash index pattern again while Zeek (Bro) is running. This should repopulate the logs, and create the new indexes using the correct default index template.

I have a few extra lines in my output config in the picture below, but you do not need those.

If you still do not get the map to show up it is because Kibana has to have an index pattern of **logstash-*** in order for it to interpret the data for the dashboards. I have repeatedly tried to duplicate issues with this process, and sometimes the Index Management Admin Panel in Kibana will make the index **logstash** with nothing else behind it. Kibana does not know how to handle an index named just "logstash." You will need to shut off Zeek (Bro), and restart services, deleted the Index, and keep trying until the log analyzer performs it's "roll-over." The easiest way I found to fix that problem is to leave the Filebeat service off, restart all other services, start Zeek (Bro), and then turn back on Filebeat. This forced Elasticsearch to use the proper Logstash naming convention. The bad part is that you can't always get the same results, so if you're having problems, you will need to play around with the services, and delete the indexes. I performed multiple steps the same way, multiple times, and got different outcomes. Elasticsearch will perform a "roll-over" with the logs periodically, and this is where I believe the hang up comes from. Once that refreshes, usually it will work, so give it sometime and keep trying to delete the indexes and restart the services until you get the proper naming convention.

Conclusion

The ELK Stack is a very versatile and powerful program for analyzing data and logs in an easy to manage centralized location. The records can be sent from anywhere and processed in one location. There are endless possibilities for how you configure ELK to handle and display your data from many different applications. There are many more uses for ELK Stack than were covered in this walk-through, but in this walk-through we covered how to install Elasticsearch, Kibana, Logstash, and Filebeat to ingest Zeek (Bro) IDS logs. Be sure to check out all the modules, and files within the ELK file folders, and you can start to get a good idea of how powerful this program can be.

Zeek Signature Configuration

In the previous sections we saw how to install and configure ElasticSearch, Filebeat, Kibana, and Logstash in order to pipeline the Zeek (Bro) Logs into an easy to manage web interface. Likewise, now that we have completed the configuration process, we can pull logs to analyze from PCAP data. Furthermore, it is equally important to create signatures that find important data that needs to be monitored. This walk-through is going to show you how to configure Zeek (Bro) to make notifications and send them to the notification or signature logs.

Today's CISOs and Cyber Security Analysts need to be able to quickly identify potential hazards, and security vulnerabilities on the network. Everything in this day and age is network centric and it's important that we can use a streamlined approach to filtering important events on our networks; the Zeek (Bro) ELK stack provides a free and comprehensive way of doing just that. Zeek (Bro) is as powerful a tool as you configure it to be. Zeek (Bro) has its own programming language that allows administrators to write their own scripts to monitor network data for detection of potentially hazardous network behavior. It's common to use a SIEM to collect high volumes of network data, but this also makes it very difficult to figure out what data is important to analyze, and what data is a false positive. Many companies spend millions of dollars on products that leave them with questions about whether data is a real threat, where it came from, when it started, and is it serious. The Zeek (Bro) ELK Stack can tell you the answers to these questions quickly and efficiently, and at a minimum point you in the right direction to start looking into potential network issues. Not to mention, ELK Stack has its own built in SIEM functionality. Wwe are going to cover that in the future. Remember, security-related issues are often missed because no one is looking for the vulnerability or because one relevant event was missed in a plethora of false positives.

Zeek (Bro) is a great tool for incident response, and network monitoring because it will give you logs that point out the data you want to quickly view, and sort. This walk-through is going to cover how to use Zeek's built in signatures and add some custom signatures that will help identify important network traffic.

Overview

- Install Zeek (Bro) Signatures from GitHub
- Listing of Signature, Notices, and Events
- Configure Zeek (Bro) after Signature Installation
- Using Zeek (Bro) and ELK stack
- Tor Traffic Analysis

Install Zeek Signatures from GitHub

1. **Run** the following command to switch to the Super User account:

sudo su

Ensure you use your Downloads folder, or whatever folder you feel comfortable cloning a repository to.

2. Change Directory to the <prefix>/Downloads folder on your machine:

cd /home/iwcdev/Downloads/

3. **Run** the following command to clone the GitHub repository containing the Zeek Site Scripts:

git clone github.com/RichardMedlin/Zeek-Bro.git

```
root@iwcdev:/home/iwcdev/Downloads# git clone https://github.com/RichardMedlin/Zeek-Bro.
git
Cloning into 'Zeek-Bro'...
remote: Enumerating objects: 62, done.
remote: Counting objects: 100% (62/62), done.
remote: Compressing objects: 100% (61/61), done.
remote: Total 136 (delta 29), reused 0 (delta 0), pack-reused 74
Receiving objects: 100% (136/136), 871.69 KiB | 4.02 MiB/s, done.
Resolving deltas: 100% (34/34), done.
root@iwcdev:/home/iwcdev/Downloads#
```

4. **Change directory** to the Zeek-Bro directory:

The Zeek-Bro directory is the directory you cloned the git repository to.

cd Zeek-Bro

```
root@iwcdev:/home/iwcdev/Downloads# ls
GeoLite2-City_20190820  geolite2.tar.gz  Zeek-Bro
root@iwcdev:/home/iwcdev/Downloads# cd Zeek-Bro
root@iwcdev:/home/iwcdev/Downloads/Zeek-Bro#
```

5. **Run** the Install file using the following command:

./install.sh /home/iwcdev/Downloads/Zeek-Bro/site/ /opt/zeek/share/zeek/

> *Note: Ensure you replaced the file path with where you cloned the Zeek-Bro repository to. You also need to ensure that you have the correct path stated for the <prefix>/zeek/share/zeek folder. This script will install the Zeek "site" folder if it isn't already there and will recursively place all the files, folders, and contents as needed. The "site" folder should exist, and the script will replace the local.zeek file and any other file that shares the same name orientation that is in the folder. So, make sure you back up any files in the "site" folder that you think may get lost when running this script.*

You will receive output showing the files were moved. Go to the destination: <prefix>/zeek/share/zeek/sites/ folder and make sure that the files were properly copied to their new location.

```
root@iwcdev:/opt/zeek/share/zeek/site# ls
basic-auth-notice.zeek      ftp-bruteforce.zeek      rdp
creditcardcaptures          http-attack.zeek         smtp
cryptomining                http-basic-auth.zeek     ssh-attack.zeek
dir-mod.zeek                http-pass.zeek           tor.zeek
dnstunnel.zeek              http-stalling.zeek       udpscan.zeek
dns-zone-trans.zeek         local.zeek
exfil-detection-framework   producer-consumer-ratio
root@iwcdev:/opt/zeek/share/zeek/site#
```

Listing of Signatures, Notices, and Events

Zeek (Bro) uses the <prefix>/zeek/share/zeek/sites/ folder to house the local.zeek file and should be used to put your custom scripts in one centralized place. The other files are located in the Zeek folders as described below. In order to make changes you need to use the " cd " command to change directory to the directory the files are in. If you have trouble locating the files by navigating through zeek you can use the command " locate " and the name of the scripts like:

locate loaded-scripts

```
root@iwcdev:/home/iwcdev# locate loaded-scripts
/opt/zeek/share/zeek/policy/misc/loaded-scripts.zeek
root@iwcdev:/home/iwcdev#
```

Ensure you use your Downloads folder, or whatever folder you feel comfortable cloning a repository to.

All of the scripts below are listed just how they are in the local.zeek file for clarity and for you to understand what scripts and signatures we are loading using the local.zeek file. Once you navigate to the folder that they are located in run the following command to edit the settings or look at the script:

nano <file_name>.<extension>

As an example:

nano loaded-scripts.zeek

Likewise, you can type the whole path that was given with the locate command like the following:

nano /opt/zeek/share/zeek/policy/misc/loaded-scripts.zeek

The following scripts are what we are going to load when Zeek (Bro) is launched and they are turned on and off in the /opt/zeek/share/zeek/site/local.zeek file. All you need to do to turn a script off is to place a # (hastag) at the beginning of the line for the script. View the local.zeek file using "**nano <prefix>/zeek/share/zeek/site/local.zeek**"and look at the example below.

Note: Notice the scripts are called by using @load and then the script folder name, or script itself. The scripts have to have a path if they are not in the <prefix>/zeek/share/zeek/site/ folder.

The following scripts have been turned on in my configuration:

```
@load http-basic-auth.zeek
@load tor.zeek
@load udpscan.zeek
@load dir-mod.zeek
@load ssh-attack.zeek

#Exfiltration Monitoring after hours add the following:
@load exfil-detection-framework
#  Redefine networks monitored for exfil in your local.bro:
redef Exfil::watched_subnets_conn = [10.211.55.0/24, 192.168.0.0/24];
#  Redefine the business hours of your network in your local.bro
#  (start time and end time must be specified on 24 hour clock):
redef Exfil::hours = [ $start_time=6, $end_time=17 ];
#  Producer Consumer Ratio for detecting PCR on the network nodes to
#  help pinpoint potential problems.

@load producer-consumer-ratio
@load cryptomining
@load dnstunnel.zeek
@load rdp
@load smtp
@load dns-zone-trans.zeek
@load creditcardcaptures
@load ftp-bruteforce.zeek
```

1. misc/loaded-scripts

   o This script logs which scripts were loaded when Zeek (Bro) was started.

2. tuning/json-logs

   o Applies the default tuning settings for Zeek (Bro) output. Remember that you need this set the timestamp correctly when using Logstash or Filebeat. If you want to use the Zeek (Bro) Module in Filebeat this needs to be changed the same way it was written up in the Elk stack walk-through. The following commands are in the <prefix>/zeek/share/zeek/site/local.zeek file:

   o redef LogAscii::json_timestamps = JSON::TS_ISO8601;
   o redef LogAscii::use_json = T;

3. redef ignore_checksums = T;
   o This setting is found in the <prefix>/zeek/share/zeek/site/local.zeek file. Enabling this allows Zeek (Bro) to ignore bad checksums. You want to do this because Zeek (Bro) will stop analyzing packets if it gets too many bad checksums.

4. misc/capture-loss

   o Estimates and logs capture loss.

5. misc/stats

   o Logs memory, packet, and lag statistics.

6. misc/scan

   o Built in script used to detect port scans on the network.

7. misc/detect-traceroute

   o This script detects traceroutes that are ran on the network. If there are a lot of traceroutes performance could be an issue.

8. frameworks/software/vulnerable

   o This script detects vulnerable versions of software on the network; usually software that is older than the current version. The default option is monitor software that is defined as local on the network.

9. frameworks/software/version-changes

   o This script is used to detect version changes, and attacker installed hard-drives.

10. frameworks/signatures/detect-windows-shells

   o This script detects forward, and reverse shells that are transmitted in cleartext across the network.

11. The following scripts detect software in various protocols as defined:

   o   protocols/ftp/software

   o   protocols/smtp/software

   o   protocols/ssh/software

   o   protocols/http/software

   o   protocols/rdp/indicate_ssl

12. protocols/http/detect-webapps

   o   Detects-webapps used on the network. This is currently disabled but can be turned on by removing the # at the beginning of the line.

   o   This script uses the <prefix>/zeek/share/zeek/policy/protocols/http/detect-webapps.sig file with detect-webapps.zeek to pick up web app traffic from major cloud services.

13. protocols/dns/detect-external-names

   o   This script shows DNS results that are outside of your local DNS zone that is being hosted externally. You have to modify the script to define the Site::local_zones variable in order for it to work.

   o   To set local zones change directory to site.zeek folder:
       cd /opt/zeek/share/zeek/base/utils/site.zeek

> *Note: You need to change the following highlighted area to contain your local zone. The second picture shows how to format the spacing and is the private address space that is just above the local zones. This gives an idea of proper spacing for the Zeek (Bro)*

nano site.zeek

```
## :zeek:id:`Site::local_nets`.  It's populated automatically from there.
## A membership query can be done with an
## :zeek:type:`addr` and the table will yield the subnet it was found
## within.
global local_nets_table: table[subnet] of subnet = {};

## Networks that are considered "neighbors".
option neighbor_nets: set[subnet] = {};

## If local network administrators are known and they have responsibility
## for defined address space, then a mapping can be defined here between
## networks for which they have responsibility and a set of email
## addresses.
option local_admins: table[subnet] of set[string] = {};

## DNS zones that are considered "local".
option local_zones: set[string] = {};

## DNS zones that are considered "neighbors".
option neighbor_zones: set[string] = {};

## Function that returns true if an address corresponds to one of
## the local networks, false if not.
```

```
option private_address_space: set[subnet] = {
        10.0.0.0/8,
        192.168.0.0/16,
        172.16.0.0/12,
        100.64.0.0/10,   # RFC6598 Carrier Grade NAT
        127.0.0.0/8,
        [fe80::]/10,
        [::1]/128,
};
```

14. protocols/ftp/detect

   ○ This script detects FTP sessions over the network.

15. protocols/conn/known-hosts

o   Tracks known assets on the network by logging hosts that have performed a full TCP handshake and logs these addresses once per day by default. This creates an easy way of seeing how many IPs are being used on the network each day. This can help identify malicious devices. The file can be modified with your parameters by using nano to modify <prefix>/zeek/share/zeek/policy/protocols/conn/known-hosts.zeek as shown below:

cd /opt/zeek/share/zeek/policy/protocols/conn/known-hosts.zeek

nano known-hosts.zeek

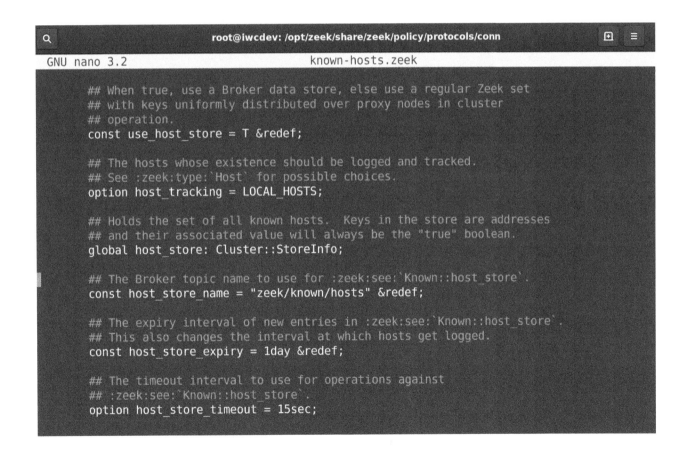

16. protocols/conn/known-services

o This script defines a service as an IP address and port that have made a complete TCP handshake with another host on the network. If it determines that a protocol was used the protocol will be logged too.

17. protocols/ssl/known-certs

o Logs the known certificates that were used on the network but attempts to discard logging the same certificate multiple times.

18. protocols/ssl/validate-certs

o This script performs certificate chain validation and caches intermediate certificates for future validation.

19. protocols/ssl/log-hostcerts-only

o This script is used to keep Zeek (Bro) from logging SSL CA certificates in the x509.log, and so that only host certificates are logged.

20. protocols/ssl/notary

o I have this turned off in the local.zeek file, but you can remove the # by #@load protocls/ssl/notary line in order for Zeek (Bro) to check each SSL certificate hash against the ICSI notary located at notary.icsi.berkeley.edu.

21. protocols/ssh/geo-data

o Logs SSH GeoIP data if GeoIP is enabled. GeoIP was enabled in the Zeek (Bro) installation in the CIR 2019 Q4 located at the following web-address:

informationwarfarecenter.com/cir/Cyber_Intelligence_Report_2019_Q4.pdf.

22. protocols/ssh/detect-bruteforcing

   o This script detects brute force attacks performed by hosts that are guessing passwords over SSH. You can adjust the following parameters by running nano and editing <prefix>/zeek/share/zeek/policy/protocols/ssh/detect-bruteforcing.zeek as shown below:

   cd opt/zeek/share/zeek/policy/protocols/ssh/

   nano detect-bruteforcing.zeek

```
## The number of failed SSH connections before a host is designated as
## guessing passwords.
const password_guesses_limit: double = 30 &redef;

## The amount of time to remember presumed non-successful logins to
## build a model of a password guesser.
const guessing_timeout = 30 mins &redef;

## This value can be used to exclude hosts or entire networks from being
## tracked as potential "guessers". The index represents
## client subnets and the yield value represents server subnets.
const ignore_guessers: table[subnet] of subnet &redef;
```

23. protocols/ssh/interesting-hostnames

   o This script looks for infrastructure hostnames used for SSH login. Furthermore, these are normally names used by nameservers, mail servers, web servers and ftp servers. Once a hostname is established Zeek (Bro) will generate a notice.

24. protocols/http/detect-sqli

- This script determines if a host is performing an SQL injection attack and will create a notification. You can make parameter changes to the file by running the commands shown below:

   cd /opt/zeek/share/zeek/policy/protocols/http

   nano detect-sqli.zeek

```
root@iwcdev: /opt/zeek/share/zeek/policy/protocols/http
GNU nano 3.2                          detect-sqli.zeek

        ## typically the body content of a POST request. Not implemented
        ## yet.
        POST_SQLI,
        ## Indicator of a cookie based SQL injection attack. Not
        ## implemented yet.
        COOKIE_SQLI,
    };

    ## Defines the threshold that determines if an SQL injection attack
    ## is ongoing based on the number of requests that appear to be SQL
    ## injection attacks.
    const sqli_requests_threshold: double = 50.0 &redef;

    ## Interval at which to watch for the
    ## :zeek:id:`HTTP::sqli_requests_threshold` variable to be crossed.
    ## At the end of each interval the counter is reset.
    const sqli_requests_interval = 5min &redef;

    ## Collecting samples will add extra data to notice emails
    ## by collecting some sample SQL injection url paths.  Disable
    ## sample collection by setting this value to 0.
    const collect_SQLi_samples = 5 &redef;
```

25. frameworks/files/hash-all-files

   - Enables MD5 and SHA1 hashing for all file transmissions.

26. frameworks/files/detect-MHR

   - This script detects file downloads that have hash values that match Team Cymru's Malware Hash Registry.
   - The registry is located at: www.team-cymru.org/Services/MHR/

27. policy/frameworks/notice/extend-email/hostnames

- Loading this script extends the: zeek:enum:`Notice::ACTION_EMAIL` action by appending the hostnames associated with :zeek:type:`Notice::Info`'s *src* and *dst* fields as determined by a DNS lookup to the Email.

28. policy/protocols/ssl/heartbleed

- This script is used to detect the heartbleed vulnerability. This bug was found and registered to the Common Vulnerabilities and Exposures Database in 2014 and is listed as CVE-2014-0160.
- This vulnerability still exists in smaller numbers, but if you do not need to monitor for it, just place a # before the @load policy protocols/ssl/heartbleed line in the /zeek/share/zeek/site/local.zeek file.

policy/tuning/track-all-assets

This script does impact performance in some cases, so if you do not need to monitor for it disable it.

- Loads the known-hosts, known-services, and known-certs policies at one time.

29. policy/protocols/conn/vlan-logging

- Once a VLAN connection is made the VLAN information is added to the connection log.

30. policy/protocols/conn/mac-logging

- Enables Link-Layer Adress logging for each end point to the connection log.

31. http-basic-auth.zeek

 o This script detects and gives a notification if there is a basic authentication
    performed over http.

32. tor.zeek

 o This script detects TOR network traffic and will give a notification showing
    which IP address was detected to use the tor network. You can edit the
    parameters of the Tor script by running the following commands:

    cd /opt/zeek/share/zeek/site
    nano tor.zeek

*Note: You can change the settings to see the best results. I currently had it set this way
for the write up so that Zeek (Bro) would trigger the notification faster. The default
settings are as follows:*

    const tor_cert_threshold = 10.0;

    const tor_cert_period = 5min;

    const tor_cert_samples = 3 &redef;

```
@load base/frameworks/notice

module DetectTor;

export {
        redef enum Notice::Type += {
                ## Indicates that a host using Tor was discovered.
                DetectTor::Found
        };

        ## Distinct Tor-like X.509 certificates to see before deciding it's Tor.
        const tor_cert_threshold = 1.0;

        ## Time period to see the :bro:see:`tor_cert_threshold` certificates
        ## before deciding it's Tor.
        const tor_cert_period = 1min;

        # Number of Tor certificate samples to collect.
        const tor_cert_samples = 1 &redef;
}
```

33. udpscan.zeek

   o   This script will create a notice if it detects a UDP scan on the network.

34. dir-mod.zeek

   o   This file monitors whatever directory is specified in line 5 of
       /zeek/share/zeek/site/dir-mod.zeek for any changes every 30 seconds. Set
       the folder path in the highlighted text below:

       cd /opt/zeek/share/zeek/site/
       nano dir-mod.zeek

```
@load base/utils/dir

event zeek_init()
        {
        Dir::monitor("/opt/test/", function(fname: string)
                {
                print fname;
                });
        }
```

35. ssh-attack.zeek

- This script is set to check for ssh password guessing and creates a notice if an SSH password attempt is generated 3 times within 60 minutes. This can be changed by using nano to edit the /zeek/share/zeek/site/ssh-attack.zeek file as shown below:

cd /opt/zeek/share/zeek/site/

nano ssh-attack.zeek

```
@load protocols/ssh/detect-bruteforcing
@load policy/frameworks/notice/actions/drop

redef SSH::password_guesses_limit=3;
redef SSH::guessing_timeout=60 mins;

event NetControl::init()
    {
    local debug_plugin = NetControl::create_debug(T);
    NetControl::activate(debug_plugin, 0);
    }

hook Notice::policy(n: Notice::Info)
    {
    if ( n$note == SSH::Password_Guessing )
      NetControl::drop_address(n$src, 60min);
       add n$actions[Notice::ACTION_DROP];
       add n$actions[Notice::ACTION_LOG];
    }
```

36. exfil-detection-framework

- These settings are found in the <prefix>/zeek/share/zeek/site/local.zeek file.
- Redefine networks monitored for exfil in your local.zeek:
  - redef Exfil::watched_subnets_conn = [10.211.55.0/24, 192.168.0.0/24];
- Redefine the business hours of your network in your local.zeek

- start_time and end_time must be specified on 24 hour clock and you can use single digits like 6 through 24 or total times like 0600 through 2400:
  - redef Exfil::hours = [$start_time=6, $end_time=17];
- Use the following command to switch to the Exil-framework folder for modifications:

  cd /opt/zeek/share/zeek/site/exfil-detection-framework

  nano main.zeek

Note: The picture below shows some of the settings you can change, but you can look through multiple scripts within the folder and make changes. This is a script that can overload some machines. You will need to try different configurations in order to tweak it to your specific needs.

```
};

## A public data structure for defining thresholds and reporting Settings
type Settings: record {

    ## How often should we poll this connection.A smaller value leads to more
    checkup_interval: interval &default=1sec;
    ## What must the byte rate be to flag it as a transfer. Note: We have fou
    ## the checkup interval or byte rate thresh, you may want to increase the
    byte_rate_thresh: count &default=2000;
    ## How many bytes constitute a file transfer.
    file_thresh: count &default=65536;
    ## Deliver this to the notice framework?
    notice: bool &default=T;
    ## Define notice type for this transfer
    note: Notice::Type &default=Exfil::File_Transfer;

};
```

37. producer-consumer-ratio

- This script is used to see which nodes transmit or receive large amounts of data on the network. This is good for finding possible malware, bitcoin mining, data theft, and many other things.

38. Cryptomining

   o This script is used to detect Bitcoin, Litecoin, PPCoin, and other types of cryptocurrency mining traffic that use getwork, getblockted, or stratum mining protocols over TCP and HTTP.

39. dnstunnel.zeek

   o DNS tunneling is a cyber-attack that encapsulates data in a DNS query or response that contains a payload that can be used to attack a DNS server. This process works very similarly to VPN encapsulation but instead uses the DNS protocol. This script detects DNS tunneling on the network and produces a notification.

40. rdp

   o This script is used to detect and notify if an event is triggered that uses RDP remote code execution vulnerability or BlueKeep denial of service.

41. Smtp

   o This script records SMTP information after decoding any base64 encoded SMTP subject lines.

42. dns-zone-trans.zeek
   o This script detects DNS Zone Transfer queries that indication recon being performed on the network and creates a notice.

43. Creditcardcaptures

- This script looks for credit card information sent across the network in plain text. The default log is redacted, but this can be altered by changing the **const redact_log = F &redef**; setting to **T** as shown in the pictures after running the commands below:

cd /opt/zeek/share/zeek/site/creditcardcaptures/

nano main.zeek

```
};

## Logs are redacted by default.  If you want to see the credit card
## numbers in the log, redef this value to F.
## Notices are automatically and unchangeably redacted.
const redact_log = F &redef;

## The number of bytes around the discovered credit card number that is used
## as a summary in notices.
const summary_length = 200 &redef;

const cc_regex = /(^|[^0-9\-])\x00?[3-9](\x00?[0-9]){2,3}([[:blank:]\-\.]?\x00?$

## Configure this to `F` if you'd like to stop enforcing that
## credit cards use an internal digit separator.
const use_cc_separators = T &redef;
```

44. ftp-bruteforce.zeek

- This script creates two notices, the Bruteforcer, and BruteforceSummary when an FTP bruteforce attack is detected.

45. http-stalling.zeek

- This script detects HTTP DoS, and DDoS attacks. The following parts of the script <prefix>/zeek/share/zeek/site/http-stalling.zeek can be changed for differing results:

cd /opt/zeek/share/zeek/site/

nano http-stalling.zeek

```
        Attacker,
    };

    ## Value representing how much time is considered too long to start and
    ## complete and HTTP request.
    const too_much_client_delay = 10secs &redef;

    ## Number of suspicious requests from an attacker or to a victim to be
    ## considered an attack.
    const requests_threshold: double = 40.0 &redef;
```

46. http-attack.zeek

    o   This script looks for non-RFC compliant HTTP requests and creates a notice.

47. http-pass.zeek

    o   This script looks for clear text passwords sent over HTTP protocol and creates a notice.

Configure Zeek after Signature installation

There are a few settings we want to configure in Zeek (Bro) before we start using the new signatures. Perform the following steps to finish configuring Zeek (Bro) for use:

1. **Change directory** to the <prefix>/zeek/share/zeek/base/protocols/ssl folder:

    cd /opt/zeek/share/zeek/base/protocols/ssl

2. **Run** the following command to edit the main.zeek file:

    nano main.zeek

Note: add port 9050/tcp to the last line of "const ssl_ports" as shown in the picture below.

3. **Change directory** to the <prefix>/zeek/share/zeek/base/protocols/http/ folder:

   cd /opt/zeek/share/zeek/base/protocols/http

4. **Edit** the main.zeek file by using thing following command:

   nano main.zeek

Note: set this option to T in order to capture the actual passwords used for Basic Authentication.

Using Zeek (Bro) and ELK Stack

This part of the walk-through will assume you have a basic understanding of ELK Stack and Zeek (Bro) after going through the other walk-throughs.

1. **Change directory** to the Zeek (Bro) <prefix>/zeek/bin directory:

   cd /opt/zeek/bin

2. **Run** the ./zeekctl command to start Zeek Control by typing:

   ./zeekctl


```
root@iwcdev:/opt/zeek# cd bin
root@iwcdev:/opt/zeek/bin# ls
bifcl     bro-config  capstats      zeek          zeek-cut
binpac    broctl      paraglob-test zeek-config   zeek-wrapper
bro       bro-cut     trace-summary zeekctl
root@iwcdev:/opt/zeek/bin# ./zeekctl
```

```
[ZeekControl] > install
removing old policies in /opt/zeek/spool/installed-scripts-do-not-touch/site ...
removing old policies in /opt/zeek/spool/installed-scripts-do-not-touch/auto ...
creating policy directories ...
installing site policies ...
generating cluster-layout.zeek ...
generating local-networks.zeek ...
generating zeekctl-config.zeek ...
generating zeekctl-config.sh ...
```


3. **Run** the Install command:

   install

```
[ZeekControl] > install
removing old policies in /opt/zeek/spool/installed-scripts-do-not-touch/site ...
removing old policies in /opt/zeek/spool/installed-scripts-do-not-touch/auto ...
creating policy directories ...
installing site policies ...
generating cluster-layout.zeek ...
generating local-networks.zeek ...
generating zeekctl-config.zeek ...
generating zeekctl-config.sh ...
```

4. **Run** the deploy command to start Zeek (Bro) with the new settings:

deploy

> *Note: Everytime you make script changes or settings changes you need to run the install and deploy commands after restarting Zeek (Bro). If everything is configured correctly in the signature or configuration files then Zeek (Bro) will launch without any errors as shown below.*

```
[ZeekControl] > deploy
checking configurations ...
installing ...
removing old policies in /opt/zeek/spool/installed-scripts-do-not-touch/site ...
removing old policies in /opt/zeek/spool/installed-scripts-do-not-touch/auto ...
creating policy directories ...
installing site policies ...
generating cluster-layout.zeek ...
generating local-networks.zeek ...
generating zeekctl-config.zeek ...
generating zeekctl-config.sh ...
stopping ...
stopping workers ...
stopping proxy ...
stopping manager ...
starting ...
starting manager ...
starting proxy ...
starting workers ...
[ZeekControl] >
```

5. **Run** the following command to check the status of Zeek (Bro):

status

```
[ZeekControl] > status
Name          Type      Host          Status    Pid     Start
manager       manager   localhost     running   29002   02 De
proxy-1       proxy     localhost     running   29053   02 De
worker-1-1    worker    localhost     running   29154   02 De
worker-1-2    worker    localhost     running   29156   02 De
worker-1-3    worker    localhost     running   29160   02 De
worker-1-4    worker    localhost     running   29162   02 De
worker-1-5    worker    localhost     running   29159   02 De
[ZeekControl] >
```

You should have a similar output as shown in the image.

6. **Run** the following commands to **stop** and **exit** out of Zeek (Bro):

   stop

   exit

```
[ZeekControl] > stop
stopping workers ...
stopping proxy ...
stopping manager ...
[ZeekControl] > exit
root@iwcdev:/opt/zeek/bin#
```

7. Set the Exfil After Hours settings in local.zeek to a time that will trigger a notification if something is downloaded on the network. Ensure you have your network IP Addresses set correctly. You will need to restart Zeek (Bro) and run the install and deploy commands.

8. Go to the Kibana Dashboard and look at Logstash logs in the discover panel. Go to the search bar and type:

   Log.file.path: /opt/zeek/logs/current/notice.log

If you click the drop down for the log, you can see a file was uploaded and detected on the network by looking at the message. The to IP address was blacked out.

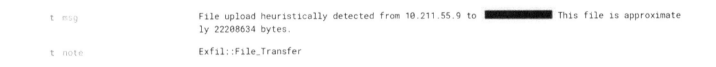

Below you will see an example of an after hours transfer notification.

t	input.type	log
t	log.file.path	/opt/zeek/logs/current/notice.log
#	log.offset	7,562
t	msg	Sent Bytes: 11178720, UID: Czykum1wHvokj6rsfc
t	note	Exfil::After_Hours_Transfer
#	p	8,080

9. Perform an NMAP Scan on your network from an external host and see what happens. You should get a notice that has a note that says Scan::Port_Scan as shown below.

10. **Change directory** to the <prefix>/zeek/logs/current/ directory:

cd /opt/zeek/logs/current/

11. **Run** the following command to view the notice.log in real time in the terminal:

tail -f notice.log

```
root@iwcdev:/opt/zeek/logs/current# tail -f notice.log
{"ts":"2019-12-02T03:13:26.222049Z","note":"Scan::Port_Scan","msg":"10.211.55.2 scanned at leas
t 18 unique ports of host 10.211.55.9 in 0m4s","sub":"local","src":"10.211.55.2","dst":"10.211.
55.9","peer_descr":"manager","actions":["Notice::ACTION_DROP","Notice::ACTION_LOG"],"suppress_f
or":3600.0,"dropped":false}
```

> **Note:** *All of the logs Zeek (Bro) generates can be viewed in the terminal, or in Kibana how we showed above.*

This is how we analyze the notice.logs and view them in Zeek (Bro). For the last part of this walkthrough we will go through generating Tor Traffic using the Tor browser we installed earlier, in the "Anonymity on the Web" walkthrough. Using the Tor browser on the network will trigger a Zeek (Bro) notice so we can ensure that the Tor.zeek script is configured correctly.

Tor Traffic Analysis

Start Zeek (Bro) and open your Tor Browser and check to see that Tor is currently working as shown in the previous "Anonymity on the Web" walkthrough. Navigate to different webpages giving time for the log shipping to catch up and then go to Kibana and look at the Notice.log.

1. When looking at the log, you will see the IP address and the message (MSG) will state the IP address was found using Tor by connecting to servers with at least 1 unique cert.

> Dec 2, 2019 @ 22:41:5 🔍 🔍   input.type: log suppress_for: 3,600 ecs.version: 1.1.0 sub: Sampled certificates: CN=www.oe57jv72f6ithflw.net
                                agent.name: zeek-beat agent.id: 668cff6f-7bd7-476b-82cd-22d16097804c agent.hostname: iwcdev
                                agent.version: 7.4.1 agent.type: filebeat agent.ephemeral_id: 798b2005-c514-4842-9757-380225b0cabf
                                host.name: zeek-beat msg: 10.211.55.9 was found using Tor by connecting to servers with at least 1 unique weird
                                certs peer_descr: manager @version: 1 note: DetectTor::Found src: 10.211.55.9 actions: Notice::ACTION_DROP,

2. If you expand the log information you will see the Sampled certificates; take note of the certificate name.

3. The next notice.log entry will have an SSL invalid Server Cert notification as shown below.

Dec 2, 2019 @ 22:41:53.101   ecs.version: 1.1.0 proto: tcp agent.name: zeek-beat agent.id: 668cff6f-7bd7-476b-82cd-22d16097804c
                                  agent.hostname: iwcdev agent.version: 7.4.1 agent.type: filebeat agent.ephemeral_id: 798b2005-
                                  c514-4842-9757-380225b0cabf host.name: zeek-beat id_resp_port: 45,647 msg: SSL certificate validation failed
                                  with (unable to get local issuer certificate) @version: 1 note: SSL::Invalid_Server_Cert src: 10.211.55.9
                                  actions: Notice::ACTION_LOG, Notice::ACTION_DROP dropped: false tags: zeek, beats_input_codec_json_applied,

4. Expand the drop down, and scroll down, and you will see the sub entry shows the same sample certificate as the certificate that triggered the Tor notification.

5. **Copy** the **IP address** and go to the following website to check if it is a Tor exit relay:

metrics.torproject.org/exonerator.html

6. Enter the information into the IP Address field and enter a date at least a day prior to when you got the notification like the below picture:

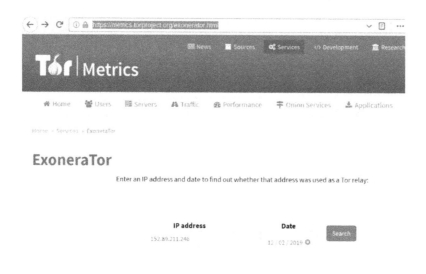

7. The ExoneraTor will come back showing if it was a known exit node or not. Some Exit Nodes are not publicly listed so it is possible that an IP may

not show on the known list of Tor exit nodes, but this gives you a good idea that there is suspected Tor traffic on the network. Likewise, this gives you a good reason to look into what may be occurring.

In this walk-through we went over how to configure and deploy signature-based scripts in Zeek (Bro). You will be able to tailor these scripts to your needs in order to find most malicious traffic that could be on your network. Being able to manipulate what you analyze on the network quickly and efficiently is critical for being able to accurately monitor network activity. Zeek (Bro) combined with ELK stack is a powerful IDS application. Likewise, this setup can be used for network analysis, incident response, or active monitoring. Using Zeek (Bro) and ELK stack to learn how different vulnerabilities trigger logs and sorting the data for quick analysis is one of the best tools you can have to become a better Infosec expert.

Kibana Visualization and Dashboard Creation

The Kibana Dashboard is used to add searches, visualizations, and maps for you to view any type of data that you ship to ElasticSearch. The dashboard gives you the ability to look at data in as much depth as you configure it to go. The dashboard itself gives you a lot of flexibility for performing analysis of information in a side by side manner. Once you make dashboards you can edit and view the data that is displayed, or you can use some of the preconfigured dashboard visualizations that are already built into Kibana. You can customize the visualizations to set up a custom SIEM to monitor events on your network. Kibana provides an interface for you to see what is happening in your network environment, and can be used to display the information in a way that is quick and easy to drill down on anomalies in system and network behavior, while also providing signature-based detection of potential malicious activity on the network.

Once you import data into ElasticSearch — using whatever method you decide — Kibana can take that data and provide multiple formats to visualize your data. You can use pie-charts, bar-charts, sunbursts, heat, region and coordinate maps, data tables, tag clouds, and histograms to name a few. Kibana allows you to add controls, radio sliders, and filters — this makes for a very versatile option when viewing data. Kibana uses metric aggregation and bucket aggregation to match search criteria in documents. Once you setup your desired dashboard panel using the visualization method, you can save the result and build a dashboard that you can access anytime.

In this section of the write-up we are going to cover how to make a Kibana Dashboard. In order to create a dashboard, you need to first create visualizations. The visualizations will be the different panes that will make up your dashboard. We are going to cover some of the basics for creating a dashboard similar to the one built for CSI Linux that can be downloaded at https://csilinux.com. Go ahead and launch ELK stack and ensure you have collected some logs with Zeek (Bro). At this point you should be in your web browser and open up Kibana by using the IP address for your SIEM.

This section will cover the following:

- Creating Visualizations for the SIEM Dashboard
  - GeoHeat Map
  - Saving Visualizations
  - Viewing the Newly Created Visualization
  - GeoIP Unique Count
  - Top Network Traffic Generation
  - Top Network Applications
  - Top Network Traffic Destination
  - Average Missed Bytes
  - Sum of Bytes
  - Notices Generated
- Building the Dashboard

Creating Visualizations for the SIEM Dashboard

GeoHeat Map

We will start by creating a heat map that shows the location of external network traffic. This will allow you to see where your network communications are coming from externally, and where your internal network nodes are sending traffic to. This is helpful for identifying malicious traffic, and you can also setup caching for your proxy server if you have one on the. Likewise, it will help cut down some of the wait times for your network nodes and allow you to optimize your network speeds.

1. **Left Click** on **Visualize**:

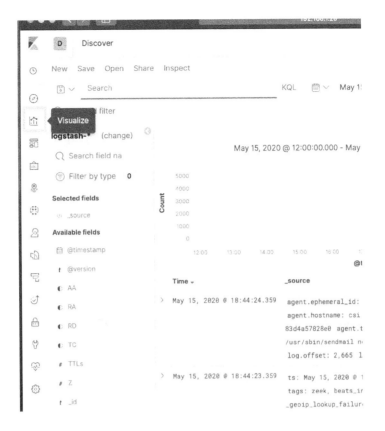

2. **Left Click** on **Create Visualization:**

Visualizations

⊕ Create visualization

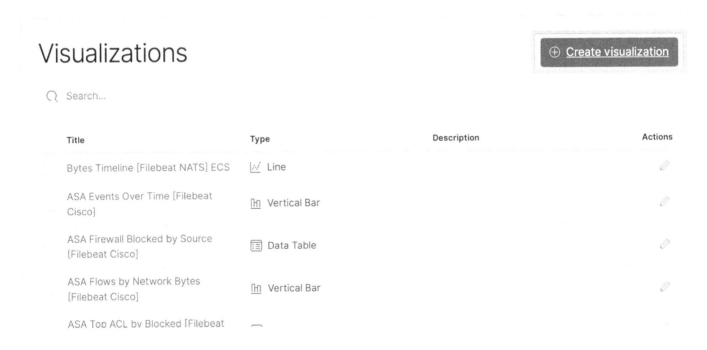

Title	Type	Description	Actions
Bytes Timeline [Filebeat NATS] ECS	∿ Line		✎
ASA Events Over Time [Filebeat Cisco]	⊞ Vertical Bar		✎
ASA Firewall Blocked by Source [Filebeat Cisco]	⊟ Data Table		✎
ASA Flows by Network Bytes [Filebeat Cisco]	⊞ Vertical Bar		✎
ASA Top ACL by Blocked [Filebeat	—		

3. **Left Click** on the **Coordinate Map** icon:

New Visualization

Coordinate Map

Plot latitude and longitude coordinates on a map

Note: Take a minute to explore the Visualization area and see the different types of panels you can create. There is a lot of flexibility for what you can do with the Kibana visualization dashboard.

---

4. **Type log** — or **logstash** and **Left Click logstash-*:**

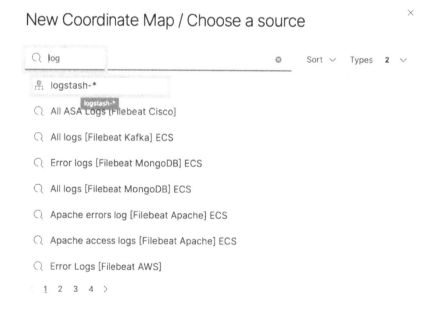

New Coordinate Map / Choose a source

5. **Left Click** the **+ Add** selection under **Buckets** and **Left Click Geo coordinates**:

6. **Left Click the Aggregation** drop down and **select Geohash — Left Click** the **Field** drop down and **Left Click geo.iplocation**, and the **Left Click** the **save** radio button as highlighted below:

7. **Left Click Options** and **Left Click Heatmap**, and then **Left Click** the **Save** radio button as shown below:

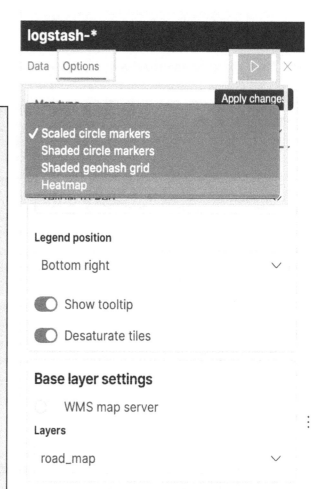

Note: If you use a WMS Map Server you can have the selected data display over that map. Just click the radio button to turn that on and enter you WMS URL, along with the appropriate layers, version, and format. Assign WMS Attribution strings, and then you can use comma separated lists of WMS Server supported styles if you use them, but you can leave that blank as well. Some servers use transparent layers, so you will need to use a png file type for the WMS Format if that is the case, or it will be transparent and will not display very clearly.

You should now have an output similar to the following. Remember, you can adjust the cluster size in the options pane if you want to make the heatmap circles larger — it is a preference for how you would like to see the heat map. Next, we need to save the Visualization — I will detail how to do that, and once you do one, you can repeat the same process each time. In the steps after this one, I will just display how to generate the visualization to save space. Refer back to the following steps to save your visualizations. The rest of these visualizations will give you a great idea of how to make your own custom visualizations. Feel free to play around with the different visualizations and create a dashboard that works for you. I will provide the basic dashboard that I found important for my setup.

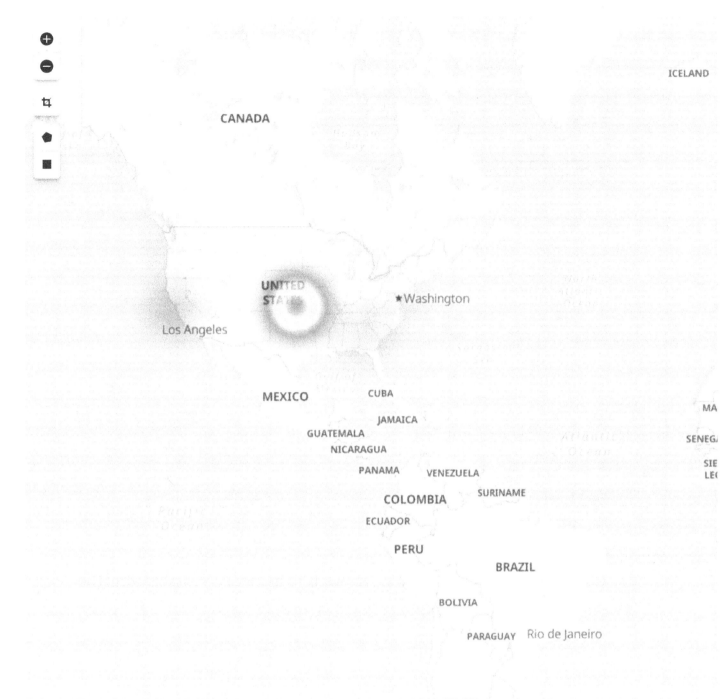

OpenStreetMap contributors, OpenMapTiles, Elastic Maps Servic

Saving Visualizations

1. **Left Click Save**:

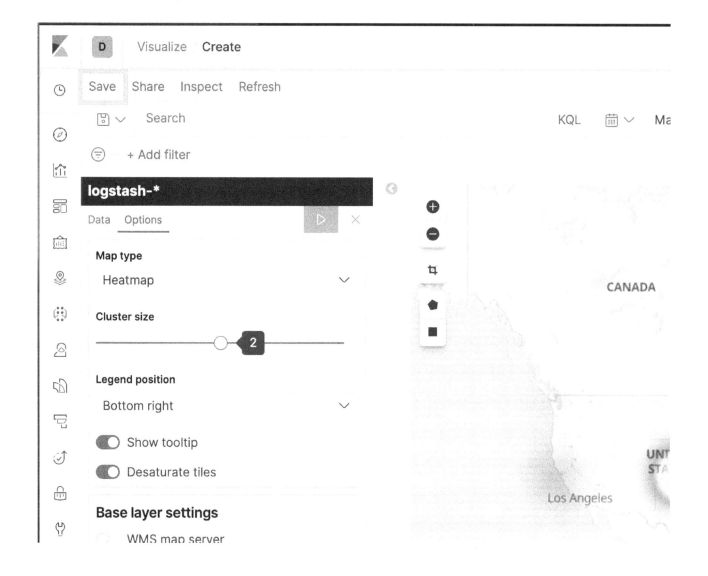

2. **Fill out** the **Title** Information that you want to name the Visualization, the **description** and **Left Click Save** in the lower right corner.

View the Newly Created Visualization

1. **Left Click Visualizations:**

You should get a pop up in the lower right corner of the Kibana page that shows saved and the name of the visualization.

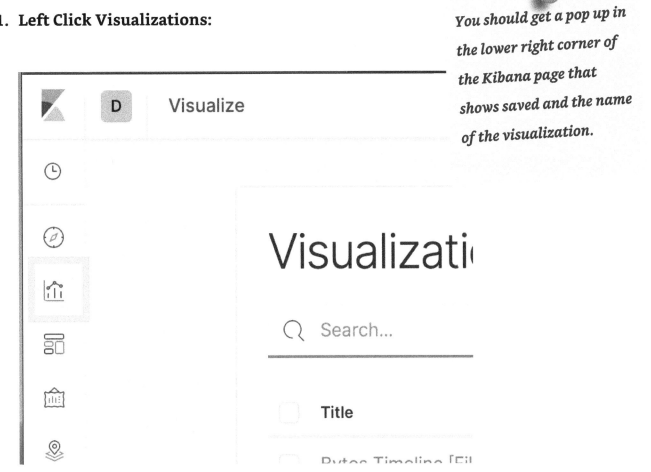

2. **Type** the name of the Visualization that you created and **Left Click** it from the list provided:

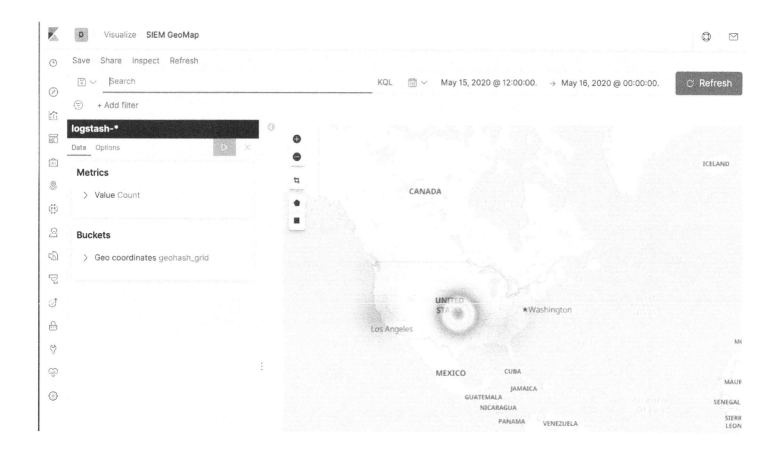

GeoIP Unique Count

This Visualization is going to allow you to show the specific unique counts of network traffic that correlates to your heat map you just created. The heatmap shows the large area of usage, while this will show specific counts based off of a color chart.

1. **Left Click** on **Visualize**:

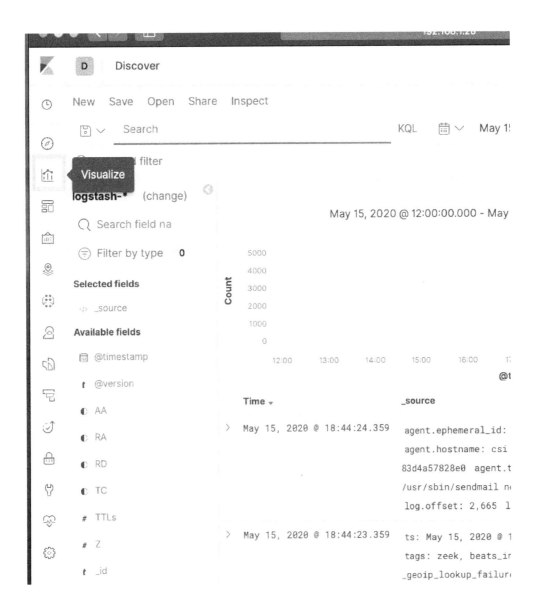

2. Left Click on **Create Visualization:**

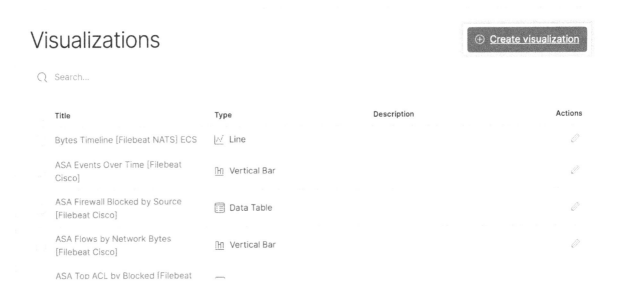

3. **Left Click Coordinate Map:**

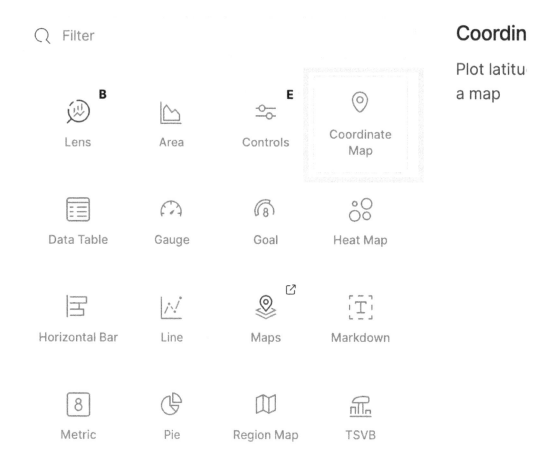

4. **Type log — or logstash and Left Click logstash-*:**

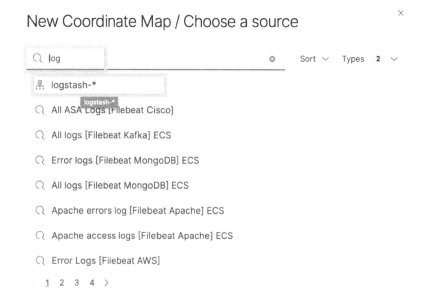

5. **Left Click the Value** drop down and **Left Click** the **Aggregation** text box, and
   scroll down and **Left Click Unique Count**:

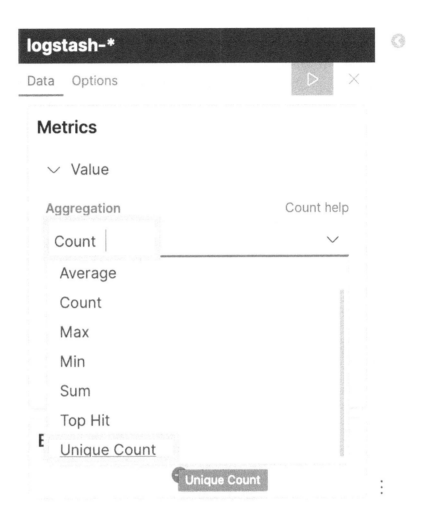

6. **Left Click** the **Field** drop down, and scroll down until you see **geo_point**, and **Left**
   Click geoip.location:

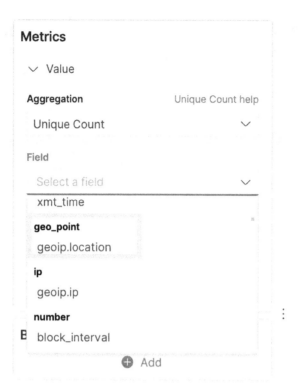

7. In the Buckets pane, **Left Click Add** and the **Left Click Geo coordinates**:

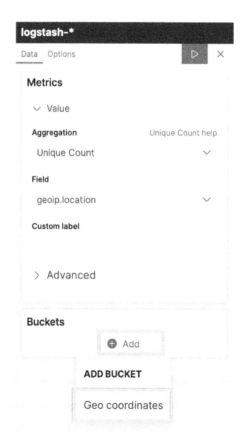

8. **Left Click Geo Coordinates** and then **Left Click** the **Select an Aggregation drop down**, and **Left Click Geohash**:

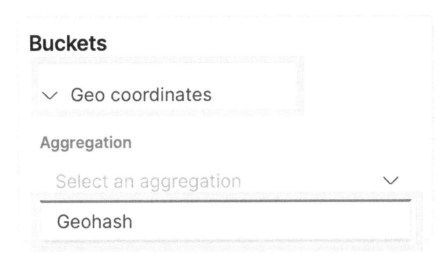

Note: *Ensure that geoip.location is selected in the Field drop down just like the heat map we created earlier. Mine was auto populated, but if it isn't just select it.*

9. **Left Click** the **Save** radio button just like the last Visualization:

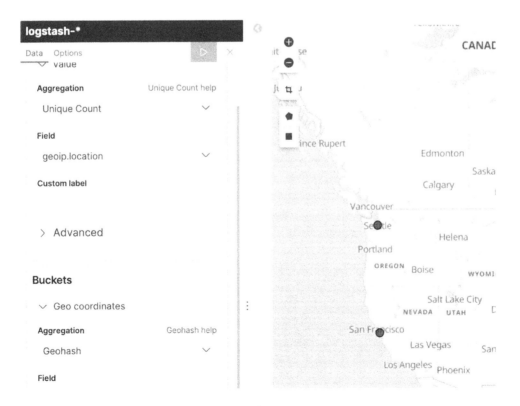

Top Network Traffic Generation

We are going to create a pie chart that can quickly show you which IP Addresses are generating the most network traffic on the network you are monitoring.

1. **Left Click** on **Visualize**:

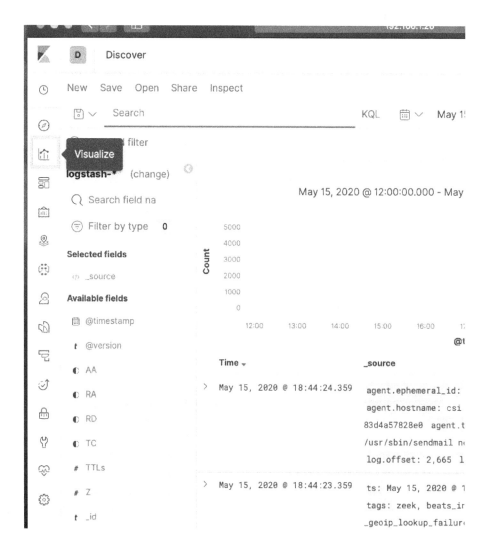

2. **Left Click** on **Create Visualization**:

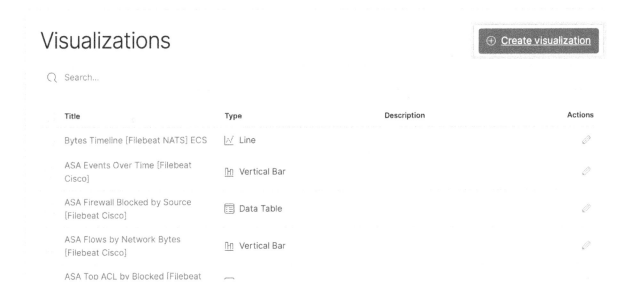

3. **Go to Visualizations**, and **create Visualization** just like the previous steps, and then **Left Click Pie**:

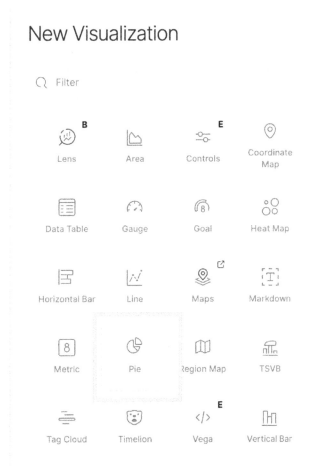

4. **Type Log** and **Left Click logstash-*** at the New Pie / Choose a source popup:

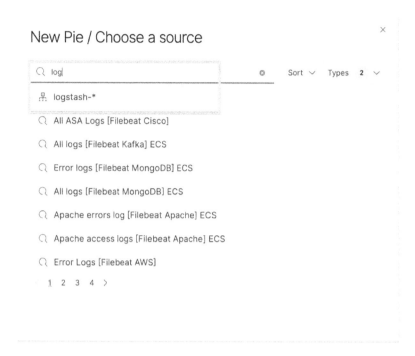

5. **Left Click + Add** — under the Buckets pane — **Left Click Split Slices**:

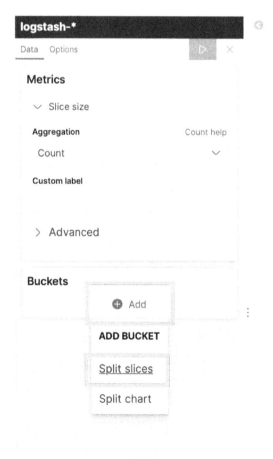

6. **Left click** the **Aggregation drop down box** and **Left Click Significant Terms** — once the Field menu pops up — **Left Click id_orig_host.keyword** — you may have to scroll down to it — and the **type 10** in under size and press return, or hit the play button for it to update the pie chart with those settings:

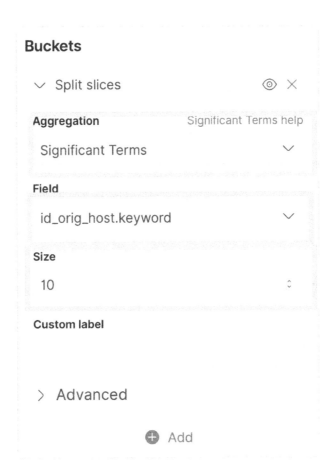

7. **Save** the **Visualization** the way we saved it in the previous steps — I saved mine as SIEM Top Network Traffic Generation.

Top Network Applications

This Visualization will show you the top network Applications based off the OSI Presentation Layer 6 data that is traversing your network. This Visualization will help you see what kind of data is being sent across the network, and what applications may be running.

1. **Left Click** on **Visualize**:

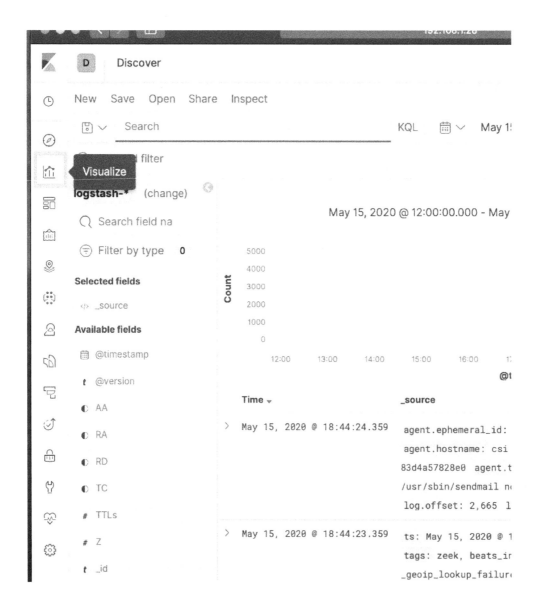

2. **Left Click** on **Create Visualization**:

Visualizations

3. **Go to Visualizations**, and **create Visualization** just like the previous steps, and then **Left Click Pie**:

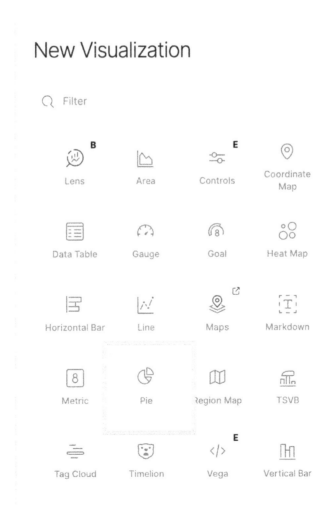

4. **Type Log** and **Left Click logstash-*** at the New Pie / Choose a source popup:

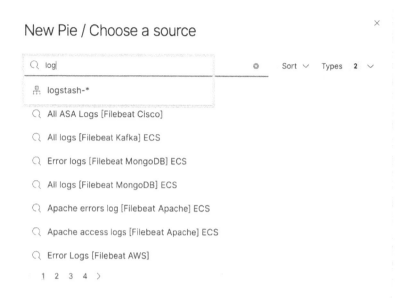

5. **Left Click** the **+ Add** selection under Buckets, and then **Left Click Split Slices**:

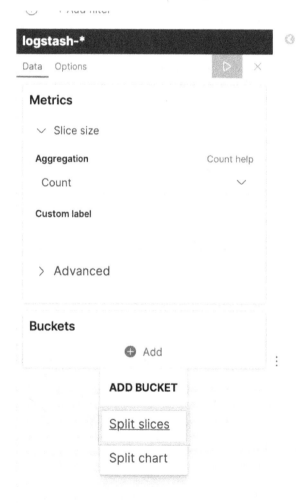

6. **Left Click Significant Terms** under Aggregation, **Left Click service.keyword** under **Field**, and **Type 10** under **Size,** and then **Left Click play** or press **Enter / Return:**

Note: *At this point you should see something similar to the above picture. I didn't generate that many logs for this example, so I'm only showing http, https, and SSL. The Size of 10 means you will see up to the top 10 presentation or session layer types.*

7. At this point you need to save the Visualization and name it — I named this Visualization as **SIEM Top Network Applications.**

Top Network Traffic Destination

This Visualization is going to show you the top Network Traffic Destinations. This is good for knowing what your big traffic producers are. When combined with the Zeek (Bro) Signature for detecting exfiltration, this can come in handy. It's also good to know because you can also tweak some network settings — if needed — to accommodate the large producers on the network for load balancing and overall throughput. You always want to have a good idea of what is generating or receiving the most traffic on the network.

1. **Left Click** on **Visualize**:

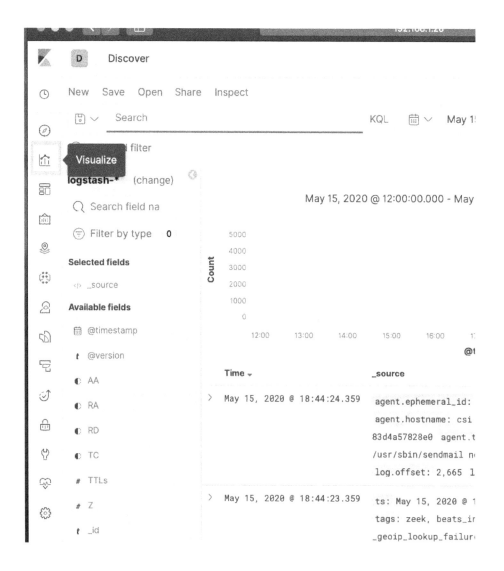

2. **Left Click** on **Create Visualization**:

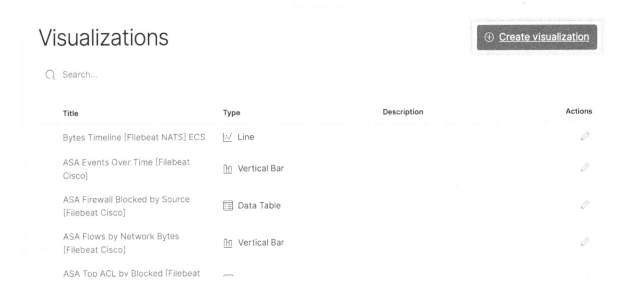

3. **Go to Visualizations**, and **create Visualization** just like the previous steps, and then **Left Click Pie**:

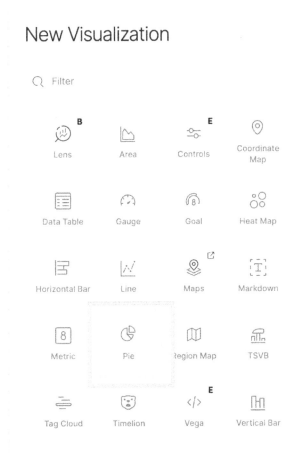

4. **Type Log** and **Left Click logstash-*** at the New Pie / Choose a source popup:

5. **Left Click + Add** — under the Buckets pane — **Left Click Split Slices**:

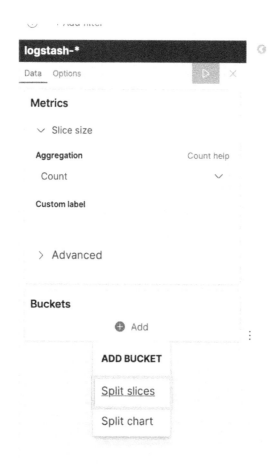

6. **Left Click Significant Terms** under Aggregation, **Left Click id_resp_host.keyword** under **Field**, and **Type 10** under **Size**, and then **Left Click play** or press **Enter / Return**:

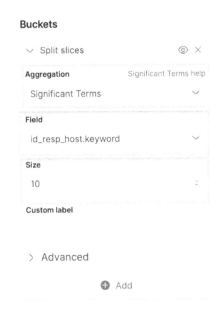

Note: You should see an output similar to the following. I am not placing the IP addresses from the top hand right corner legend, for privacy.

7. At this point you need to save the Visualization and name it — I named this Visualization as **SIEM Top Network Traffic Destinations.**

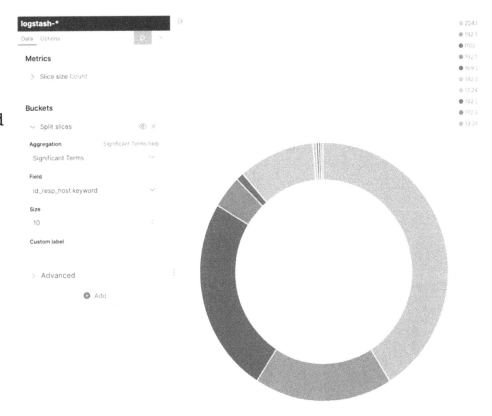

Average Missed Bytes

This Visualization will show you a gauge that uses metrics to determine if your SIEM / IDS is dropping any network packets. You do not want there to be a high number here, because that means something is not working right. This will allow you to trouble shoot any issues that could arise and will quickly point out that something is wrong.

1. **Left Click** on **Visualize**:

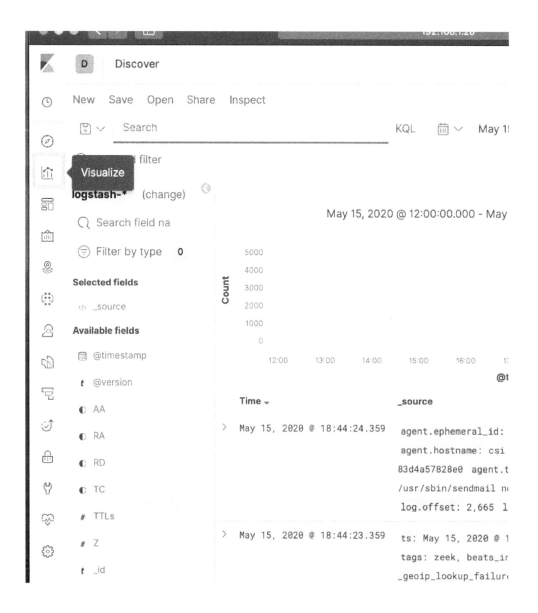

2. **Left Click** on **Create Visualization**:

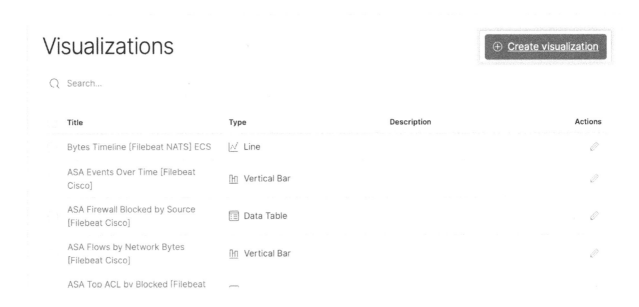

3. **Go to Visualizations**, and **create Visualization** just like the previous steps, and then **Left Click Metric**:

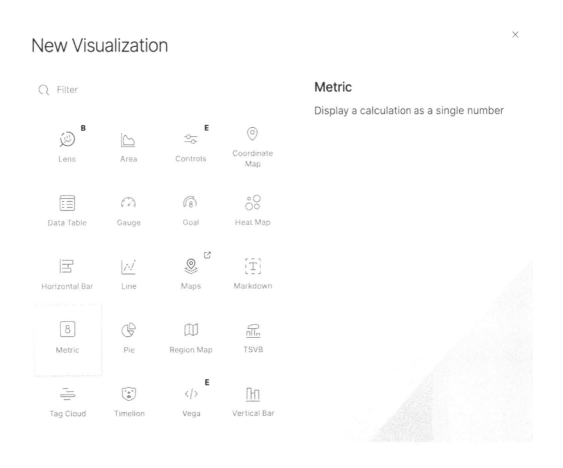

4. **Type Log** and **Left Click logstash-*** at the New Metric / Choose a source popup:

5. **Left Click Aggregation** drop down and **Left Click Average**, **Left Click Field** and **Left Click missed_bytes** and **Left Click** the **save** radio button:

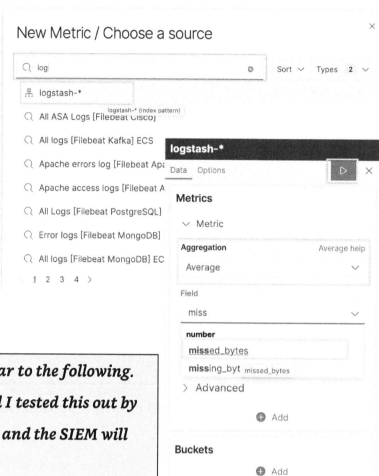

Note: You should see an output similar to the following. Zero missed bytes is a good thing, and I tested this out by making some tweaks with Zeek (Bro), and the SIEM will pick up if anything is missing.

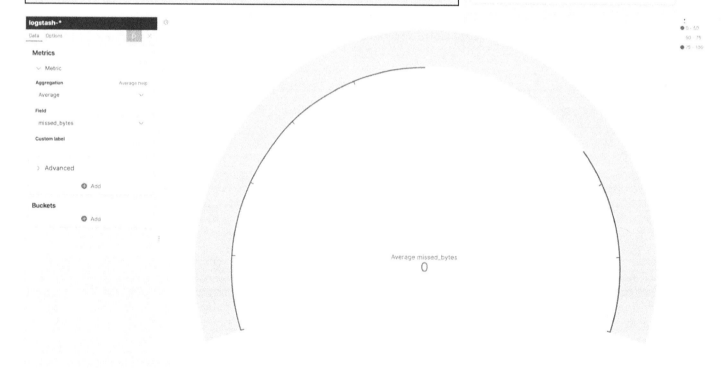

Sum of Bytes

This Visualization will show you the total Sum of Bytes captured on the network. It's important to quickly see that your SIEM is working and capturing traffic, and this metric allows you to do just that.

1. **Left Click** on **Visualize**:

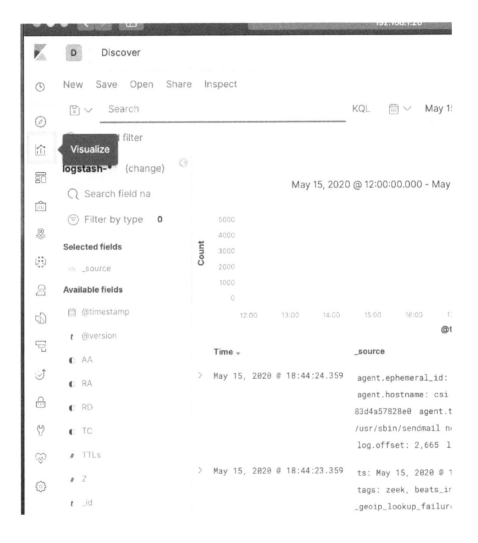

2. **Left Click** on **Create Visualization**:

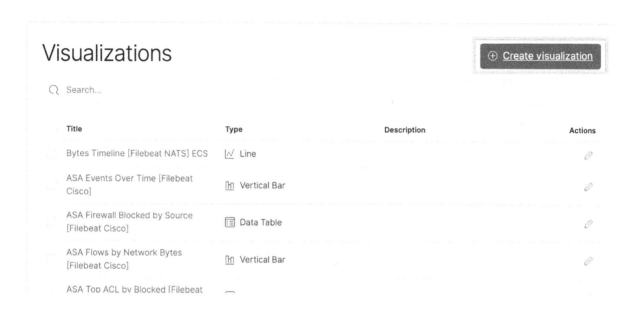

3. **Go to Visualizations**, and **create Visualization** just like the previous steps, and then **Left Click Metric**:

4. **Type Log** and **Left Click logstash-*** at the New Metric / Choose a source popup:

5. **Left Click Aggregation** drop down and **Left Click Sum**, **Left Click Field** and **Left Click total_bytes** and **Left Click** the **save** radio button:

You should get an output similar to the following picture.

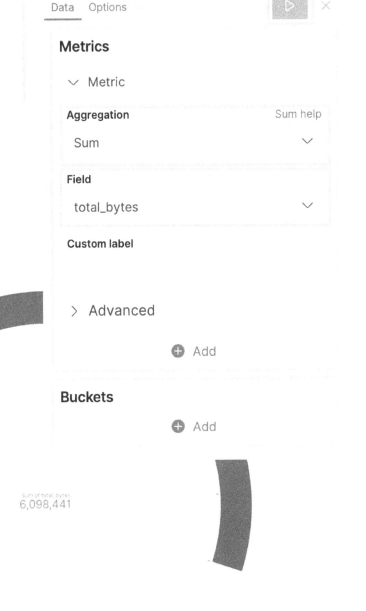

New Metric / Choose a source

Q log

| logstash-*
Q All ASA Logs [Filebeat Cisco]
logstash-* (Index pattern)
Q All logs [Filebeat Kafka] ECS
Q Apache errors log [Filebeat Apache] ECS

logstash-*

Data   Options

Metrics

∨ Metric

Aggregation   Sum help

Sum   ∨

Field

total_bytes   ∨

Custom label

› Advanced

⊕ Add

Buckets

⊕ Add

Sum of total_bytes
6,098,441

Sum of total_bytes

Notices Generated

This Visualization is one of the most important ones you will have — notices generated by Zeek(Bro). This is a quick way to show you how many notices have occurred. These notices are generated by Zeek (Bro) when it detects an anomaly on the network — signatures are used to generate the notices and you can use many different kinds of signatures for whatever reason you choose.

1. **Left Click** on **Visualize**:

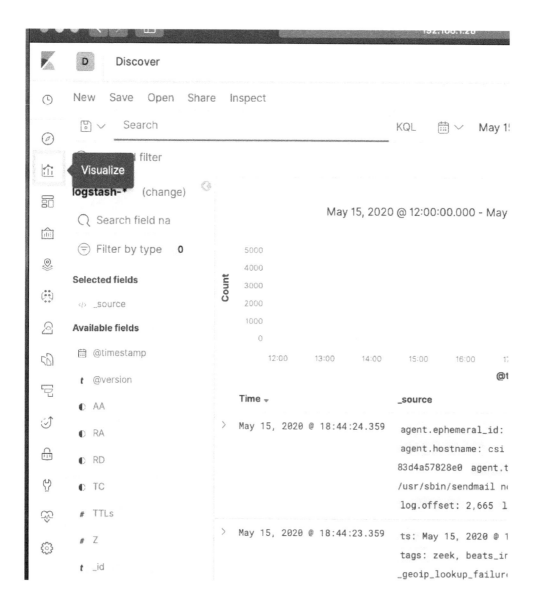

2. **Left Click** on **Create Visualization**:

3.

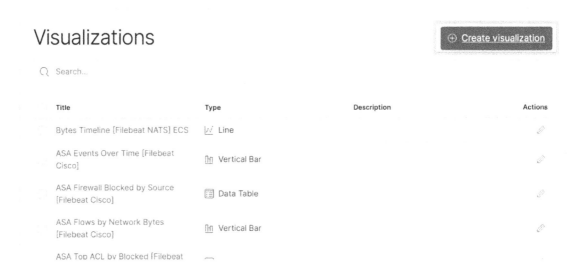

4. **Go to Visualizations**, and **create Visualization** just like the previous steps, and then **Left Click TSVB**:

5. **Left Click** the Color Box that is green, and make it a color you want to stand out — I chose red:

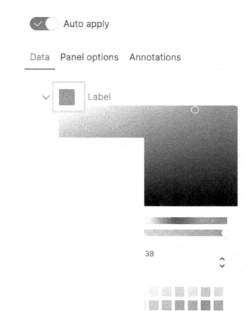

6. **Left Click Label** and type **Notices**:

You can put any label name on your network and make another Time Series metric for that. This is useful for looking at specifics over time.

7. **Left Click Panel options** and **Type** the following under **Panel filter:actions.keyword :***

The final output for this Visualization should look similar.

Mouse over on the data points to see the count of notices at any particular time you highlight.

Building the Dashboard

The Dashboard is an important tool for looking at information in your SIEM. It is essentially the view of your SIEM and built from Visualizations. You can build this however you want, and you can use any visualization you choose. In the following steps I am going to show you how to create your own dashboard. I had previously setup a dashboard for CSI Linux, so I will be using the Visualizations from that just to make it easy, and show what CSI Linux has available — it's a great digital forensic tool, and can be located at https://csilinux.com.

1. **Left Click** the **Dashboard** icon:

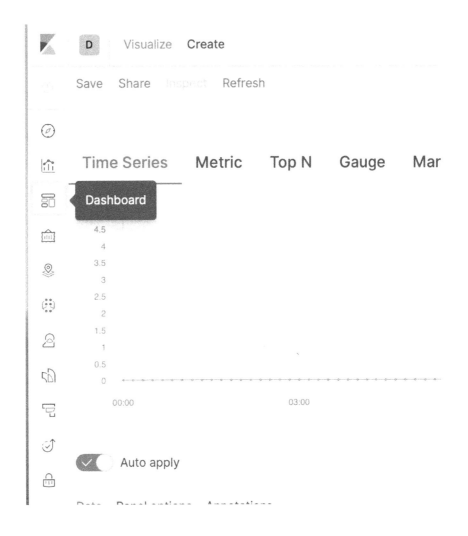

2. **Left Click Create Dashboard**:

Dashboards

Create dashboard

Q Search...

3. **Left Click Add**:

This dashboard is empty. Let's fill it up!

Click the Add button in the menu bar above to add a visualization to the dashboard.

If you haven't set up any visualizations yet, visit the Visualize app to create your first visualization.

Note: You will get an output similar to the following. In order to move the panes around just click the top portion in the area where I highlighted, and you can also drag the dotted edges and re-size the panes. You can arrange this area any way you like, play around with it and see how you want it. You can click add up top and add more panes too.

- 188 -

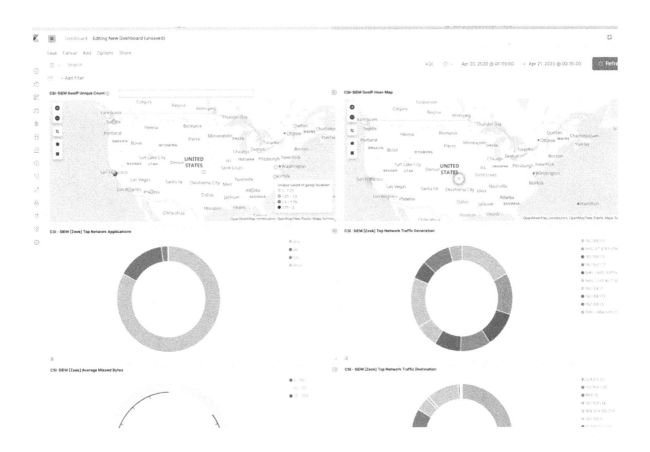

I added a highlighted box to the corner where you need to drag in order to re-size the panes as follows:

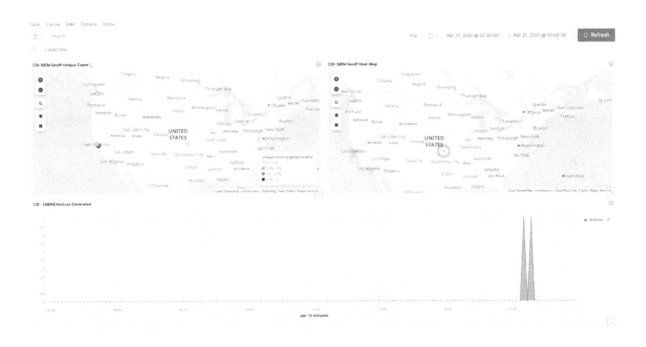

Now your dashboard is complete, we need to save the dashboard.

Saving the Dashboard

1. **Left Click Save:**

2. **Left Click** the title and **Type** the title you want to use, and **Left Click Save:**

Now when you go to the Dashboards menu you will see your dashboard:

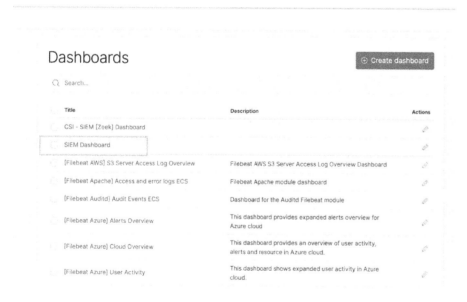

Conclusion

That concludes the entire ELK Stack SIEM process. We learned how to set up Zeek (Bro), PF_Ring, ElasticSearch, Logstash, Filebeat, Kibana, and creating a SIEM Dashboard. I challenge you to continue to create and modify your ELK Stack and use it to the best of your ability. This SIEM is a very powerful setup, and there is a lot of flexibility in how you implement your signatures, the data you capture, and how you manage your SIEM. This guide will help you get started and, on your way, to monitoring your network!

If you want a prebuilt solution or a "SOC in a Box" CSI Linux is a great solution. I have helped build the Incident Response and SIEM environments along with the Tor Gateway environment. The SIEM gives much of the capabilities that we have discussed in this book, along with a bit more. This is a constantly evolving security and investigation system that is designed to minimize your efforts and maximize your results.

Below is a section that specifically talks about CSI Linux so you can judge for yourself if it is right for you. If you do decide to try it out, the team is always open for suggestions to make it better for both you and your team.

Cyber Investigations
CSI Linux – CSILinux.com

We believe that having the right tools to do the job is critical for forensic investigators. That is why we have created a multi-purpose, all inclusive, investigation environment starting with online investigations (OSINT, social media, domain recon, and dark web) to offline Digital Forensics Incident Response to Malware Analysis and more. This is an ideal environment for both training and real-world investigations.

What Makes this different than the hundreds of other options out there? Well... CSI Linux was developed by Computer Forensics, Incident Response, and Competitive Intelligence professionals to meet the current needs for their clients, government, and the industry.

CSI Linux Investigator is a Virtual Machine Appliance that contains 3 different virtual machines. CSI Linux Analyst is the environment that you will use most of the time. CSI Linux Gateway is a Tor gateway that can help mask your online location while allowing the tools within CSI Linux Analyst access to the Tor dark web. CSI Linux SIEM contains the tools you need for identifying local network threats. All three can be used together or in combination with other Virtual machines.

The first challenge that we focus on is the ability to minimize the time and effort it takes for reconnaissance and Open Source Intelligence (OSINT) analysis. The Internet is a goldmine of useful data. Tracking a suspect? Want to know what hackers know about you? Need to link user accounts to prove collusion? These are some of the challenges many of us face every day. We are making this easier and cheaper than ever before.

The second challenge we face is the cybercrime case... If a hacker or even an Advanced Persistent Threat (APT) is your target of investigation, how do you catch them? What do you do once you identify the threat? Welcome to the world of incident response and network forensics. With a combination or state of the art technology and good old-fashioned investigative know-how, we are working on a low budget solution for making your cyber triage and emergency response easier and more streamlined.

The third challenge is malware analysis. You may never need this, but if you come across an application or process that seems malicious and none of your security solutions are catching the activity, we have you covered with our SIEM that includes Elasticsearch, Kibana, Zeek IDS, and other incident response tools. Once you identify the suspicious code, you can use Radare 2 and the NSA released tool Ghidra to investigate further.

The fourth challenge is the classic computer forensics also known as "Dead Box" or Postmortem" forensics. There are a ton of options out there and we are working on the ability to tie all 4 challenges together into one standard solution.